FINDING *the* NARROW PATH

Patterns, Faith and Searching

FINDING *the* NARROW PATH

LIN WILDER

Finding the Narrow Path
Lin Wilder

FIRST EDITION

ISBN: 978-1-942545-54-5
Library of Congress Control Number: 2016942228

Copyright © 2016 Lin Wilder
All rights reserved.

No part of this book may be reproduced or transmitted in any form or by any means without the written permission of the publisher, except in the case of brief quotations used in book reviews and critical articles.

Wilder Books
An Imprint of Wyatt-MacKenzie

Finding the Narrow Path is dedicated to Almita Bey-Carrion and to all those who struggle with the questions of faith.

∼

But small is the gate and narrow the road that leads to life, and only a few find it. (Matthew 7:14)

So you are no longer aliens or foreign visitors: you are citizens like all the saints and part of God's chosen household. You are part of a building that has the apostles and prophets for its foundation and Christ Jesus himself for its main cornerstone. As every structure is aligned on him, all grow into one holy temple in the Lord, and you too, are being built into a house where God lives in the Spirit. (Ephesians 2:19)

ACKNOWLEDGEMENTS

THE LIST OF THOSE who were instrumental in teaching me about the need for and direction to find faith is far too long to enumerate in this short book. I know people who claim the presence of angels in our lives. Not the spirit angels but humans who appear providentially, for a particular purpose. Perhaps that explains the mystery of virtual strangers, who assert spiritual knowledge or can accurately predict events in our lives. Such as my long ago Freshmen English teacher at Hunter College. Or Joanne Wessman, then Professor of Nursing at Oral Roberts University, whom I met while living in Tulsa and who perceived the depth of the spiritual battle I was fighting and perplexed me each time she expressed her understanding of it. And who later authored a splendid chapter on stress and its role in cardiac disease in my textbook, *Advanced Cardiovascular Nursing*. One which caused more than a little consternation among a few of the medical doctors who contributed to the book.

Or the Anglican Pastor Brian Clench whom I met in Cornwall, England when he claimed he could see the intensity of my spiritual struggle and predicted it would resolve, leaving firm faith in its stead. And fleeting relationships with others through the years who would baffle me when they said similar things. Like business acquaintance Nan Goddard, who merely smiled and nodded almost nonchalantly after I confided at a business dinner in Worcester, that I had become a Roman Catholic. Surprised by her lack of surprise, I was speechless and wondering. Nan noticed my open mouth and the stunned look on my face. She explained, "David and I have been praying for you for years, Lin, we knew that God had his hand on you and that it was only a matter of his timing, my Sister in Christ."

But several people must be recognized because their contributions to my life and this book are too vast to be overlooked. My husband John, my spiritual partner from that very first seven-hour telephone conversation, I thank you for the constancy of your need to grow in the love of God and His wisdom. And for your clarity. And for your decision to marry me. All of my spiritual directors but especially Fathers Greg, John, and Paul.

The brothers and priests at St. Benedict's Abbey in Still Water Massachusetts, especially Brothers Andrew, Bartholomew, and Abbott Father Xavier. Sister Marie Bernard and John Bradshaw, former teachers at Dominican College in Houston, Texas, both of whom who shared their immense love of learning and thinking prodigiously. After all of these years, their impact on the direction of my life resounds. Dr. Andy Papanicolou, former Department of Neurosurgery, University of Texas Medical School at Houston, without your guidance, friendship and help, I would not have made that trip to Greece alone, specifically Delphi. I would never have known about the rock that Zeus split. Dr. Stephen Linder, former advisor and Chair Dissertation Committee at the University of Texas School of Public Health in Houston, Texas. The years of study with you were an honor. Your advice and friendship during those very challenging weeks of my last summer in Houston were invaluable. Margaret Caddy, my friend from day one at

Dominican College, Susan Toscani, Almita Bey Carrion, thank you for your willingness to read and comment on the first iteration of this manuscript. Cate Baum, thank you for your excellent editing. Nancy Cleary at Wyatt-MacKenzie, once again you nailed it. Kudos to you for your visual genius.

Thank you to all who were kind enough to comment honestly on this cover, especially those of you who advised against this one because it is 'too churchy.' After a good deal of reflection, I realized that the Church is a lighthouse for this battered, tortured world. Considered passe, even obsolete by many of the seven billion souls on the planet, She remains the sole means of reaching Truth: Jesus. The only way to join with our brothers and sisters in Christ.

A MESSAGE TO THE READER

I TOLD MY FRIEND Margaret that this was the hardest writing of any I've ever done as I got close enough to the end to see it done. "Can you imagine discovering the most precious gift of your entire life? One that changed everything and yet keep from making it a rant?" This is a story about how and why I lost faith in God. Since I did not return to faith until midlife, there were a few decades crammed full of multiple tries to achieve what only faith could provide me. They were years of confusion, riddled with errors in judgment, some of grave consequence. Years in which I believed in nothing, subscribed to no religious maxims and considered myself an atheist or agnostic. Hence, the two chapters titled 'Lost Years.' Despite the fact that I spent half my life in school, and much of the rest trying to figure out the answers to the variety of pressing issues of my career, I know far too little to claim the real knowledge or wisdom I thought I would find in all those years of education. We go after advanced degrees for a variety of reasons: A ticket to a job or for training which can be obtained only in specific programs are the most common reasons. To introduce us to some of the greatest minds and teach us how to reason may not be expressed in words but for some students, that is a more fundamental goal. It was certainly mine. And if fortunate, as I was, we are taught not what to think but how. A most crucial distinction.

I loved the years spent in my undergraduate and my doctoral programs. Far too much I realized when I was done with both of them. Positive that the answers to the questions which I could not put into words lay in education, I was flattened by what I did not feel upon graduation from both: Wise. Only twenty-four at the time I graduated from Dominican College in Houston, Texas, I solved my problem by getting married. But twenty-five years later, when I completed my doctorate, I hit the wall. Finally, I had learned, the answers to the questions which haunted me could not be found in a degree, title, a place or a man. Writing from the fifth century, St. Augustine expresses the timeless call:

You were within me, but I was outside, and it was there that I searched for you. In my unloveliness, I plunged into the lovely things which you created. You were with me, but I was not with you. Created things kept me from you, yet if they had not been in you they would not have been at all. You called, you shouted, and you broke through my deafness. You flashed, you shone, and you dispelled my blindness...

CHAPTER ONE

Introduction

WRITING THIS ACCOUNT OF my return to faith and conversion to the Catholic Church was not my idea. A non-fiction writer for many years, to my great surprise, I fell in love with writing fiction. The creative freedom within fiction and the constant challenges imposed by both old and new characters in my novels had long ago captured my heart and mind. My plan was to revise the manuscript for my third novel, *The Price For Genius* to ready the book for a spring 2016 release and then move on to the fourth book in this series of books featuring characters whom I have grown to love. The overall plot for the new book excited me, and I was eager to begin. Until I remembered a promise made several years ago.

"Lin, there is no way I can understand how you feel about your faith, your relationship with Christ and the Catholic Church. These are things I have had all my life. I have never known a life without them. In a sense, I take them very much for granted. But when I listen to you talk about your faith, it's as if I am listening to a love story... You fell in love, didn't you?"

Indeed.

Acknowledging my silent agreement with her statement, my

dear friend Almita Bey-Carrion continued. "I know you are loving writing these novels, I get the joy this work brings you but I want you to make me a promise." Her dark brown eyes were intense, the expression on her face suddenly serious.

Concerned and unsuspecting, I put down the forkful of spinach salad down and stared at my friend. We had met for lunch at a small restaurant and Almita's sudden gravity was out of character, I was afraid something was wrong with her or with a member of her family. "Of course, I'll promise you anything… if it's something I can do."

"I want you to promise me that you'll write your story. Write a book about your journey back to God. How can I or anyone else understand this love you have been given unless you talk about it, write about it so that others can see what you see?"

I was taken aback by her request. In fact, I was trying to figure out a way to say "No, I cannot do this, even for you." Talking to a good friend about hugely private matters was one thing. But putting this at times most unpleasant and disturbing story into a book for strangers to read was something else again. I did not like the thought, not at all. Antsy and uncomfortable, I waffled several times in attempts to evade making a commitment. So I danced around the answer she wanted using phrases like, 'let me think about it', 'not sure this is a place I want to go' and hoped she'd let it drop.

Characteristically undeterred, my friend insisted. "Yours is a story which must be told." The intensity of her gaze undimmed, Almita said, "Lin, I believe God is using me to convince you to get your story out there. Others need to read what happened and how this happened. I *know* that many will be touched, inspired by your journey." Her dark brown eyes were huge, the intensity in them seemed to spark. "I don't care when you do it. I understand you are excited about this next book you're finishing now.

I get that. But *please*, promise that you will write this story of yours, Lin."

Grudgingly, I agreed. And promptly forgot the promise.

Until the beginning of this past Lent in 2016. For the entire first week, I could write nothing. Despite the fact that I had a self-imposed deadline, I could not force myself to work on the novel scheduled for a spring release. And I had tons of work to do to get the book in shape following the first read from my editor. But I could not write a word, or even think about it.

I know writers who work according to strict schedules like a regular work day from nine in the morning ending at five. They work solely in an office primarily designed for their writing and treat their writing as work days. This does not work for me. I can write only when I know the words are there, waiting to be released.

Over many decades of writing, including failed attempts to meet critical deadlines, I have learned that I cannot force it. When the impetus, flow, and or inspiration are absent, extorting words from an empty well will produce only drivel. At these times, the only solution is the obvious one. Don't write. Wait.

Finally, ten or so days into the forty days of Lent, I remembered the promise made to Almita several years ago. And I knew suddenly that this book needed to be written before I could return to my novels, recognizing the source of my 'block' finally.

CHAPTER TWO

Lost Years Begin

"IT'S A BURDEN BUT also a blessing to walk away from the faith of your childhood and family. You are one of the rare few who will one day find a faith which is your own, not the religion of others but uniquely *yours*...more important than any other thing in life, perhaps one you would be willing to die for."

The speaker taught Freshman English to night-school students at Hunter College in New York City, where I worked nights full-time and attended college part-time. I do not remember his name. He wrote poetry under a pseudonym for the New York Times, stood on the top of his desk while portraying Falstaff and saved my life one night after class.

I have no idea what impelled my twenty-one-year-old chaotic self to ask my English teacher for help. Or what prevented him from begging off to go home to his undoubtedly waiting family at nine-thirty that April evening after a very long day of teaching. But he did not do that. Rather, he led me into his office, sat down behind his desk and peered kindly at me.

Before I could get more than a few words out, the deluge of tears prevented any coherent conversation for five minutes, at least so it seems in my memory. We sat in his tiny colorless basement office while I collected myself enough to be able to explain why I was there, crying my heart out, in front of a virtual stranger. Patiently, he listened to a tale of a young woman from a small Massachusetts town who had moved to New York City to work nights in a cardiac ICU while in pursuit of 'wisdom' at college. Who no longer believed in Jesus. Or religion. Who could no longer call herself a Christian. Who had failed in multiple attempts to explain the awful day she sat in a pew at the Cathedral of St. John the Divine Episcopal Church on Easter Sunday with friends. Hung over, barely able to focus on walking, never mind prayer, during the service, then walked out into the way-too-bright sun where reporters from the New York Daily News stopped her and her two friends to take pictures of "three lovely young women on a beautiful Easter Sunday in New York." While her friends posed and smiled for the photographers, delighted and flattered, she could focus only on the nausea and headache, trying not to be sick and embarrass her friends. And realized she had lost her faith. It was gone. Vanished as completely as if it had never been there in the first place. Leaving only a huge and hollow void.

Despite a visit back to that same church a few months later in early December, where I sat alone in the cavernous Cathedral, hoping that this dark and ominous feeling would go away, it did not. Looking around at the cross, the crèche with the Christ child, Mary, and Joseph in front of the altar, the magnificent trappings of the church, it was as if I were looking at signs and symbols of an alien race. These made no sense to me. How fervently I wished that I could once again join my friends on Sunday mornings at church and then Sunday brunch at The Tavern on the Green. But everything I had been taught as a child had devolved to myths and lies. I could no longer attend church. Or celebrate Christmas. Or call myself a Christian. Jesus was concocted, a man who had never existed and the Bible a fairy tale. The hypocrisy would be impossible, the fakery too massive.

I tried to talk with my friends and family about what felt like a horrific, appalling loss, their response varied from laughter and condescension to a perplexed silence. However, it was the accusation of a close relative that my break with church and God derived from a desire to "be like every college student, needing to appear like an intellectual" that provided the impetus to seek help. His words echoed in my heart and mind, long after they had been said, I was tormented by the mockery and his patent mistrust that my decision to stop attending church had been reached through any legitimate process. Perhaps he was right, maybe these dreadful feelings of godlessness are artificial, intended only to impress.

Certainly I had been playing around with religion and faith for a number of years, reading books like Nietzsche's *Beyond Good and Evil* and Bertrand Russell's, *Why I Am Not A Christian*, much of which I barely understood. But faith is like any habit. It must be exercised and must grow through prayer, study and a personal relationship with Christ. I knew nothing about any of these things. Yet, stupidly, I had never reckoned for this abyss. My confusion, loneliness, and devastation were profound. I felt like I was going crazy.

Until I heard these words. Heard him- this college professor- say that he too had left the faith of his childhood. That he had been Jewish but stopped believing and, like me, could no longer attend synagogue because it was hypocrisy, he could not bear the pretense. And so he withstood the rage of his father, the mute incomprehension of his mother.

"I broke their hearts," he said with tears in his eyes. "But I could not do it; I could not behave like a believer when I was not."

It wasn't just that he believed and sympathized. He *under-*

stood. He had, perhaps still was, living my experience. He changed everything for me that evening. He gave me hope.

So many times through the years I have thought of this man, the immensity of his kindness, wisdom, and solace. And wished I could contact him to tell him the depth of the impact he made that night. The preciousness of the gift of his time and his heart to an unknown night student. A person who should have meant only papers to read and grade.

To reveal the end of the story, the unmitigated *rightness* of his prediction: 'One day, you will have a faith that is yours. That cannot be taken from you. That is yours. That is more important than anyone or anything.'

But I don't remember his name.

CHAPTER THREE

Growing Up

DECIDING TO WALK AWAY from God did not come easily or quickly. Nor did the decision to return. These kinds of tumultuous events feel as if they happen impulsively, spontaneously. But, if we take the time to look back at patterns, we find the seeds of the decision sown years before the actual action. Lee, my oldest sister, said she was unsurprised when I called her in Houston to tell her that I'd become a Catholic. When I asked why, she asked, "Don't you remember that we called you Sister Mary when you were a kid?" I didn't, but she reminded me of my excessive demonstration in religious matters as a child, the genuflections, making the sign of the cross and other sacramentals that fit better with Catholicism than with our Episcopalian religion.

Smiling, Brother Andrew said, "October 7, Lin, your birthday is the Feast of the Holy Rosary." Incredulous at the thought of the guidance and direction shining on the twists and turns of my life which led here, I gazed dumbfounded at him. Brother Andrew was the Benedictine monk who spent the summer of 1996 teaching me the foundations of Catholicism, readying me to receive the sacraments enabling me to join the Church.

Because of childhood illnesses, some of which threatened my life, I don't remember much of my early years. Perhaps because of the multiple hospitalizations, I was a withdrawn and fearful kid throughout most of childhood and spent lots of time alone. I learned early that when someone in a white coat said it wouldn't hurt, they didn't mean it. It took years for a recurring nightmare where I was standing in a crib-like bed, watching my father walk away down an endless hallway through the bars of the crib to disappear.

The source of the Sister Mary allusion by my sister was the decision to send me to camp when I was ten or eleven. My parents hoped that six weeks at the summer camp would result in more confidence and a better ability to socialize with other kids of my own age. But the camp was run by Anglican nuns, dressed in starched habits, indistinguishable from the Catholics. These women fascinated me as did their mystical and mysterious practices. The silence and accouterments of devotion. I came home with the ambition to become a nun and spent the rest of the summer talking with a Catholic neighbor about her faith, asking her endless questions until my mother put a stop to it. Exactly how that happened, I no longer remember, but my parents were not happy with the results of the summer camp experiment.

By my beginning teens, my mom recognized the gravity of her youngest daughter's timidity and reticence and worked with me on almost a daily basis using books by Norman Vincent Peale to build up my self-confidence. She was indomitable in her conviction that this withdrawn, insecure and introverted kid could change. Remarkably, over those few years when neither of us wanted to continue the reading and studying of *The Power of Positive Thinking*, *The Art of Real Happiness*, and *A Guide to Confident Living*, Mom's determination bore fruit. I changed, radically.

I have many regrets about my relationship with my mother.

But expressing my gratitude to her for the insight and sacrifice of these daily sessions where I was forced to read aloud, even memorizing parts of Peale's writings is not one of them. Through the years of adulthood, up until her death, I wrote and told her how thankful I was. And to explain just how thoroughly mindful I was of the magnitude of the change in my personality that had been wrought by her insistence. My mom was not a psychologist; she'd had two years of secretarial education after high school. The fifties in America was not a time of self-help nor were there many resources for a woman concerned about her child. How, where and why she got the idea to do this, I do not know. But she changed me.

In my late teens, when the predictable rebellion revealed itself, I would frequently jibe my mother for evoking an oversupply of self-confidence in her youngest daughter. Enough to generate exceedingly annoying behavior. For example, the Saturday afternoon when she walked out into the back yard to find me reading Bertrand Russell's, *Why I Am Not a Christian*. Her single comment was a mild, 'I guess you won't be coming to Sunday services tomorrow.'

Mine was an ordinary family. Mom stayed at home to care for her three daughters while my father worked grueling jobs with hard physical labor. By the time I was born as the last of the three girls, my dad had his own business, first a gas station and then a steam cleaning shop, which guaranteed loads of grease filled work clothes. And hands which were never quite cleaned of black oil and lubricants. Pretty much a constant source of annoyance to my mother who seemed obsessive about cleaning her house.

During those early years when I was mostly solitary, it was Sunday walks with Dad and the dog which were the highlight of my life. He and I talked about all kinds of things. Everything from life in outer space to the meaning of life. Things my mother had neither the patience or interest in, she was intensely practical. Mistakenly, I interpreted her unwillingness to converse about ideas which fascinated me as a lack of intelligence on her part. Dad was my model, the person I most admired and felt closest to.

Religion was a Sunday affair but only for our mom and us girls. Dad did not go to church. His childhood memories were filled with Saturday night brawls followed by Sunday confessions in his poor mostly Catholic neighborhood of South Boston. If either of my parents prayed, it was a private event. We did not say grace before meals nor was God or religion discussed in any way other than a cursory manner. But ours was a fairly typical American lower- middle- class family of the fifties and sixties. Although not said often, morals were clear as were expectations of us. Things like no sex before marriage, honesty, respect for all and the value of work were implicit in our family.

Our mother determined that her daughters would have a way of providing for themselves, most likely because she had been forced to quit her job when she became pregnant with my oldest sister. I always thought her economic dependence on our Father chafed at times. Dad was plainly very proud of his two older nurse daughters, keeping their nursing graduation pictures prominently displayed at his workplace. This was a huge factor in my decision to attend nursing school also despite the vigorous objections of my mother who knew with the uncanny prescience of mothers that I would dislike the rules, regulations, the whole set up of hospitals, doctors, and nurses. Which, of course, was wholly right.

From the very first day as a student nurse on the medical floor, I hated it and begged to quit. I had asked a question of the Head Nurse about a patient I had been assigned. I don't remember whether I did not agree with a doctor's order for the man or a belief that he needed something that had not been ordered, I can vividly recall the look on Ida Hooper's face when she saw me approach to tell her that I thought. Mrs. Hooper had flaming red hair and a temper to match. When I did not go away but repeated my concern using different words, believing that she must not understand what I was asking, her face grew as red as her hair, and she began to shout. Something like, "Miss Carney, do you not understand what doctor's orders are? And that your job is to follow them?" I didn't, not if I thought the order wrong.

Rightly, my mother explained the numerous times she had advised me not to go to nursing school and the fact that tuition had been paid. I had started something. It was important to finish what we start. All valid, reasonable statements. And so I stayed there, studying as little as possible, getting into as much trouble as possible, a first for the girl who had been mostly anonymous in high school.

One of the surprises of those three years was the friendship of the 'popular girls.' My two best friends had dated throughout high school and were accustomed to boys and bars, unlike me who knew nothing of either. So it came as a bit of a shock when boys and young men liked me, thought I was pretty. And I enjoyed it. But I desperately missed the conversations with my father and was disappointed when my dates had no interest in those kinds of intellectual pursuits nor did my friends. The 'trouble' I got into was relatively innocuous, caught smoking in the dorm, staying out past the curfew, things most girls had done in high school.

That part of the three years was fun. The remainder was an endurance test. There were several more incidents with faculty members similar to the one with Mrs. Hooper, and I suspect that there was a building file on me, with plenty of critical comments by faculty members. There was one instructor, a woman named

Pat Furze, who saw something in me. Actually liked my questioning, did not think it rebellious or arrogant and would engage me in conversations about whatever it was that I opined about. I recall her saying that if I could manage not to be thrown out of the school, she could imagine my making real contributions to nursing.

When, during my senior year, we spent three months in the brand new specialty of critical care, things changed. For the very first time, I was interested, challenged, even excited. But not enough to consider changing my plan.

As soon as nursing school was over, I focused on what I thought of as a *real* education-college. What my mother had wanted for me all along. This time, I knew better than asking my folks to help me financially so I scrimped and saved money while working in the then new field of cardiovascular critical care, first at Mt. Sinai Hospital in New York City while studying at Hunter College. Then at St. Like's Hospital in Houston while studying at Dominican College, a small private Catholic women's college. Ironic isn't it that the college where I was awarded a full-tuition scholarship was a private Catholic college? My intention was to leave nursing once I figured out how to do something important, help to change the world.

CHAPTER FOUR

The Early Years

SINCE MY CONVERSION TO Catholic Christianity, I have done numerous talks for groups of all ages, composed of people from all walks of life- from moms and housewives to priests and to teens. Most of my listeners have been lifelong Catholics or Christians and have not experienced living life without faith. Frequently, in attempting to convey what that is like, I would stamp my foot on the hard wooden or cement floor to which I stood in front of them. And say there is no ground to stand on. Everything is possible for someone without faith. Everything is permissible, nothing is prohibited.

One of the many problems with very specific and time-limited goals is the question of what one does once the goal is met. I graduated from Dominican College on a rainy day in June. And found myself crying in despair for all the exact same reasons as I did many years later while sitting on the steps of the University of Texas School of Public Health having completed my doctorate. The goals were met, what now?

Because I had disliked nursing school so intensely and loved my hard-won undergraduate studies with equal intensity, I expected to *feel* something once the undergraduate degree had been conferred. Working while going to school is not the most difficult task we face, far from it. But it is not easy. Time becomes a precious commodity, one which must be allocated carefully, precisely. Work pays the bills. Therefore, it automatically gets priority leaving only non-work time for attending class, study, writing papers. And social life? A distant third place.

But I loved the introduction to the thinkers who shaped western civilization. Meeting great minds like Plato, Socrates, St. Thomas Aquinas. Studying under the head of the English Department at Dominican College, Sister Marie Bernard, the first woman I ever held in awe, was pure privilege. For me, she was an iconoclast as she smashed many of my previous ideas of religious rigidity and narrowness one by one.

Unaware of the oxymoron she seemed to personify, during my first class with her, she assigned us Edward Albee's play, *'Who's Afraid of Virginia Woolf?* This remarkable woman passionately incited us to think, question, and reason past the shock of the epithets of the screenplay.

Later that semester, she assigned atheist Robert Bolt's *A Man for All Seasons,* a play which became a favorite for life. One which I have read and re-read, introducing me to a long-ago man, Thomas More, the man who seemed like the antithesis of a saint. Lover of life, good food and wine, the very reason that Bolt called him a man for all seasons. This was a man any of us could identify with, one who attempted every possible compromise with Henry VIII because he wanted to live, had no interest in racing to his death. No one could read the play without wondering just exactly what defined her so completely that she was willing to die rather than compromise that boundary.

I never saw Marie Bernard without that habit. The starched white material of her headpiece seemed to imprison her forehead and cheeks, almost painfully. But this woman permitted no locked doors to her mind or those of her students if they could listen. Her joy was in sharing her love of literature, all of it. I remember listening to her lectures about Faulkner, Eliot or Auden, wishing I had her knowledge of the Bible. Aware that I was missing a huge foundation of knowledge, perhaps even the wisdom I sought so earnestly.

On very few occasions, I conquered my veneration for her enough to go and talk to her after class. Always she was kind, warm and welcoming. And exceedingly complimentary about my writing. She astonished me when one day I asked when she had entered the convent. Lips turned up with that Mona Lisa smile of hers, she replied that she had been thirty-five when she entered. Adding that she had owned a successful bookstore which had been very hard to walk away from. Had she always been a Catholic? Did she ever have doubts? Had she ever walked away from God? Exceedingly curious, I was filled with questions like these and many more, but something stopped me from asking even one of this very private woman. After all, since she had never broached the subject of my lack of faith, how could I ask her about her exceptional devotion?

I no longer remember how I learned that Sr. Marie-Bernard had completed her Ph.D. in English Literature, but recall only that I was unable to let such a momentous event pass without ceremony. Feeling weird when I knocked on her office door with one hand and balancing an enormous cake on which was written in frosted capital letters, Congratulations, Dr. Marie-Bernard, relief saturated me when I saw the grin of pure pleasure which split her face in two. She looked like a child as she cut the cake, insisting that I sit and eat a piece with her.

Sacred Heart Dominican College was the sister Catholic school to University of St. Thomas, then exclusively male – and the only school for certain classes like philosophy.

Morning classes began with Mass, a Latin ritual which I sat through uncomprehendingly. Although my lack of participation was noticed and commented on by a few of the nuns, never once did I sense any judgment from Sister Marie-Bernard. Nor did she ever use what she had to know was a considerable influence on me to preach.

Long after my return to faith, I asked Margaret, a close friend since the very first day I set eyes on her in the coffee shop at the school, if she thought Marie-Bernard had prayed for me back in those days. Such a close friend who, although herself a Christian, always listened and accepted my doubts, conflicts and frequent war with God without judgment. Another who never preached. Without hesitation, Margaret replied, "Well, of course, she would have." I like that thought.

The first time I saw the light that no one else sees, it was Margaret and only she whom I spoke with about it. I was in a philosophy class at the University of St. Thomas watching the Monseigneur diagram St. Thomas Aquinas' Hierarchy of Being on the blackboard right next to where I sat in a class with about thirty-five other students. The priest spoke rapidly, with a thick accent and firm conviction. Standing in his long black robes, his right hand started at the bottom of the board, in broad sweeping strokes of the chalk on the blackboard, wrote, "Archangels," above that "Principalities" and then "Virtues" on to the "Seraphim." The entire board was covered.

I sat staring at the words, wholly uncomprehending them. It felt as if I were looking at an alien language. And began to ponder while gaping at the board that this was an absolute fabrication, none of this existed, there was no God. But there was none of the sarcastic teen I had been before in my thoughts. None of the wisecracking quoter of Nietzsche's "God is dead, he choked to death on Theology" that I parroted on frequent occasions mostly to achieve the satisfying shock the comment generally elicited from my listener. There was just despair, pure and black. And I sat wondering if it just would not be far simpler to end all this. The more I considered the idea of suicide, the faster the bleak thoughts flashed through my mind.

When abruptly, the entire window lit up. I was seated right by the blackboard, five rows away from the wall of windows which were so bright that I was convinced that it had finally happened. Russia had dropped a bomb. World War III had begun.

But the Monseigneur continued to stand by the board and drone on about the Seraphim. And all of my classmate's heads were bent toward their notes as if assiduously taking down every word out of the priest's mouth. Only then did I realize that no one in the room saw what I did. In awe, I sat watching the brilliance which lit up the entire wall of windows. My heart rate accelerated, and the blackness and suicidal thoughts disappeared entirely leaving something which I could not name, but I knew it, almost recognized it. Then a powerful impression of peace enveloped me, almost like a blanket. That night, I went home and wrote a poem. I called it the Divine Spark, a tiny light which existed somewhere in me, somewhere deep but there and connected me to something I could not name. That was the first time I saw the light. There would be others.

There was another teacher there who profoundly impacted the way I thought and questioned life and what I wanted out of it. No stranger to grief, disappointment and error, John Bradshaw had left St. Michael's College Seminary at the University of Toronto just days before his ordination as a Catholic priest. Apparently deeply troubled, confused and mourning his lost vocation, Bradshaw applied to Sacred Heart for a teaching job. The Dominicans had no problem hiring this passionate young man who was no longer Catholic, maybe even an agnostic. Too anxious and confused myself to notice Bradshaw's obvious contradictions and flaws, I took every class he taught, excited by the man's appetite for learning, for a mind which liberally spilled out quotes from everyone from Santayana to McLuhan, several of which still serve as maxims for my life. Still, I can picture him shouting "most people live in the basement of a three-story house" and challenging us to 'LOOK at that tree!"

John Bradshaw seemed to love teaching in that unpretentious tiny college. Or at least, if he did not like what he was doing, he faked loving it with every fiber of his being. Many times at particularly dark periods of my life I have recalled his stomping through the classroom admonishing us about happiness. "If you want to be happy, *act* like you're happy, do the things you would if you *were* truly, deeply happy, *say* the things that a profoundly happy person would say." And then smiling broadly, "Suddenly, to your great surprise, you realize, by God, I AM happy!" Nonchalantly, he would toss off quips like, "I'm jealous of the angels. They don't need eyes to see, ears to hear or a brain to learn...ZAP, they just KNOW." And I would sit there, thrilled by his hope, determined joy and thinking about angels. Differently from the academic hierarchy of philosophy class but for the very first time in my life, wondering about beings who never need to eat or sleep. Was it possible they actually did exist?

One afternoon, on the way home after that day's classes were over, I pulled my car to the side of the road, parked it, got out and stood to look at an enormous tree. And worked to do exactly what Bradshaw advised. And *look* at the tree, see it, even be it. Working full time and taking a full-time load of classes required a discipline and a rigid schedule. My study time was precious because I did not have a lot of it. I had an unpleasant problem that I knew I needed to deal with. I could not afford an apartment in a nice part of Houston without a roommate, even then I could afford just one bedroom. And since I knew Jeannie would be there when I got to the apartment; I dreaded going home. But I had a German exam the next day and had to study, hard.

Jeannie was, in a word, strange. She would sit on the other twin bed in our small bedroom and stare at me while I studied. If I moved into the living room, Jeannie followed me and continued her bizarre habit. Many times I complained, begging her to go do something, anything but she claimed there was nothing she would rather do than watch me study. With startling green eyes, Jeannie's gaze was eerie and unsettling. Standing by the tree on that hot, humid afternoon, I decided to deal with this. So what if I had to live in a dump in a less than optimal part of Houston. And I hoped that my brother-in-law and his friends would help me move again. They did. Within a week I was out of there, living alone in a far older, smaller and less impressive apartment. But it was relatively safe. And I was able to study.

On Sister Marie Bernard's suggestion and gentle encouragement, I took the Graduate Record Exams and applied to Graduate School for English Literature. When I received the letter of acceptance from Fordham University for a full-tuition scholarship for their combined Masters through to Doctoral Program, I was scared to death. This would mean leaving the life I had built in Houston, moving again, and acting on the childhood dream I'd had of writing a novel. I could not do it. I chickened out and turned down the offer, pretending to myself that I could not leave Bob, the thirty-five-year-old stockbroker I was dating. And told no one I had done it, not even her.

Now that I had turned away from a career in university life and decided to stay in what I claimed I disliked, nursing, I felt adrift, disappointed in myself and confused. Feelings which would return with vengeance many years later on completion of my doctorate in public health. All that sacrifice should mean something. And a degree so passionately pursued should confer a sense of pride, accomplishment if not wisdom. But none of those emotions or anything remotely resembling them was present, only a deep understanding, close to shame and embarrassment, that I had no clue of what to do with my life.

It feels more than a little strange to confess these facts because the motive behind much of education is, fittingly, a ticket to a job. Exactly as my wise mother had counseled her three girls. Because as women, one of our primary goals is a natural one, wives, and mothers. Certainly that was true for most of all the women I knew then and throughout my life. But not for me.

A watercolor print called "Our Battles Are Many" is prominently displayed on my bedroom wall. I found it in a southwestern store in Houston and fell in love with what it said to me. The painting depicts two profiles and one full face image of an Indian warrior. Under the faces and profiles in what would be the neck and torso of the soldier are ten or so small penciled sketches. Each one representing a lone warrior engaged in battle. I felt as if I were staring at my life, openly displaying the skirmishes, combat, and occasional wars. I keep it today as a reminder of all those years without God. When I had no faith other than the latest seer I'd discovered, long before I recognized the 'God-shaped vacuum' in my heart.

Patterns are best seen by looking in the rear view mirror. Mine were formed early: ambition, a determination to live a life different from my mother, one without marriage or husband along with a deep and lasting confusion about being a woman. Conflicts about how to integrate being female with being ambitious. About men, sex, children. The determination to *succeed*. Although I never considered myself a feminist, I fought a long lonely and painful battle about the tensions between wanting to be popular like my two older sisters and the fear of living their lives. Where marriage and motherhood were the primary goals. And where education was merely a fallback- important just in case.

Once while watching my mother iron, I brilliantly said, "I'm not going to waste my life like you did, I'm going to be famous." I was seventeen or eighteen at the time.

Serenely, without stopping the strokes of her iron on the garment, most likely one of mine, my mother smiled. If she said anything, I don't remember what it was.

Exactly how much of my personal life should be included in this book has been a tough decision to make. This is, after all, the story of a conversion, not an autobiography. Many of my choices, judgments, and their consequences remain painful, even humiliating to revisit, writing them down, even more so. Initially, I questioned the relevance of describing elements of my career, education and relationships with men- in short, my pre-Catholic world in detail. Since I did not convert until midlife, there are a lot of territories to cover. But I realize that my use of the term 'lost years' makes no sense unless I place them squarely in the context of the person I was then. Without the details of my early life, unpleasant as they are to recall, much less write, this sense of drifting and of aimlessness are merely words which lack substance. They are unidimensional. In talks to church groups about life with and without my faith, I frequently used 'ground' while I stomped the floor I stood on, forcefully, as I worked to convey what is gained and lost with and without faith.

Faith and all which accompanies religion like regular church attendance and a belief that there is something greater here, someone present, informs our decisions and choices, even our goals. Just so, its absence widens all boundaries. More and more is acceptable. By my early twenties, I had adopted the mantra of the times, the infamous sixties, and discarded the prohibitions to sex before marriage more out of curiosity than passion or romance and had a few 'one night stands,' liking myself less and less after each one. I believed that the line between what was permissible and impermissible sexually was outmoded now that women were 'coming of age' in the world. Worse, I refused to consider just what was making me feel dirty after intercourse with a man I cared little about. After all, I reasoned, men were culturally encouraged to experiment sexually, why was not the same 'freedom' appropriate for women?

In an article called "Our Battles Are Many" for a Catholic Women's magazine published shortly after my conversion, I wrote this, "My battles were representative of the tremendous cultural changes occurring during those years. They were waged in an internal, private, and bloodless war deep within me."

But now as I think about those early years, I believe the truth to be simpler and far less flattering. I got caught up in the most banal of human sins, pride, and in my own lies. Pride in my wish to avoid the powerlessness and boredom of women's work like child bearing and raising. And the many lies that I told myself about men, marriage, and relationships. Twice, I disregarded the warnings of friends about dating two men who insisted to me that they were single but were in fact, married with children. Upon discovering their lie, I protested their interest in me but weakly enough that I allowed my conscience to be trodden one more time. The second of these two married men, I married after a long and tumultuous divorce.

My first husband and I would never have married had I been clear about who I was or what I wanted. But at the age of twenty-five, I was a jumble of mutually exclusive behaviors. Displaying an outward image of confidence and flirtatious ways I had learned during my late teens and early twenties in response to the surprise of men finding me desirable, I acted like most young women of the late sixties and early seventies. Looking for a man with whom to settle down, make a home and raise a family. But nothing could have been further from the truth.

Critical care medicine was new, exciting and challenging. And Houston, Texas was where medical history was being made by a surgeon named Denton Cooley in the Texas Medical Center. Here was a setting in which a young, aggressive nurse could operate on an almost level playing field with doctors if she were eager to learn and willing to study. Using borrowed medical textbooks from one of the leading Cardiologists in the country at the time, I developed the first course for nurses working in the Cooley Critical Care Unit. Back in New York, while working at Mt. Sinai Hospital, I had taught myself how to read the cardiac monitor by borrowing another textbook. The Chief Cardiology Resident at Sinai found my questions about basic electrophysiology so interesting that he lent me one of his textbooks and by the time I left for Houston, I knew what I was seeing on the cardiac monitors, what it meant and how to treat it. In fact, my knowledge almost got me fired one night. It was there that my lifelong love-hate relationship with rules matured.

There were very few patients in the unit that Sunday night, therefore, I was there alone when suddenly, one of my patients named Tilly coded near the end of my shift. I called for the Code Team as I was supposed to do. But minutes went by without a response, and I knew she was in ventricular fibrillation. She would be dead without treatment. So I defibrillated her, twice. By the time the code team arrived, she was in normal sinus rhythm and breathing on her own.

The Day Supervisor for the entire building stopped me as I stepped out of the elevator to go home, get some sleep and get to class at Hunter. The unsmiling and starchly uniformed woman, complete with cap, asked that I follow her into her office. Taking a seat behind her desk, she looked at me and declared that Mount Sinai nurses were not allowed to defibrillate patients. That was a medical procedure and could be performed only by licensed doctors. Did I not know this? I explained what happened. That I knew the patient would die if I did nothing. And the Supervisor repeated that I did not have the authority to do what I did.

To her credit, the woman kept her cool for the entire twenty minutes that this went on. Me, disheveled and smelly after my harrowing shift, standing in front of her desk with her sitting there, crisp, starched and capped, I guess trying to figure out what to do with me. Finally, I said something like this. "I badly need to brush my teeth, the patient vomited into my mouth when I first began mouth-to-mouth, and I have classes this afternoon at Hunter College. I understand the need for policies and procedures but don't you think they can be only guidelines? Because that patient would be dead if I had not done what I did. And she is up there doing fine." Apparently, the entire Code Team had been stuck in an elevator. Thankfully, I refrained from asking her why no one had praised me for saving the life of this patient. Finally, she let me go home.

The rigorous, intensive study of borrowed medical texts of cardiovascular physiology and pathophysiology was all-consuming and exhilarating. One of the leading cardiologists in the country, if not the world, took a personal interest in me. Dr. Hall spent many hours explaining the most obscure sections of his textbooks on which I based the course I was creating. Once more, I fell in love with the learning, the seduction, even power, of knowledge. And with the perfection of the cardiopulmonary system and its compensatory mechanisms. The more I learned, the more Dr. Hall piled on me, treating me just like he treated his medical residents.

For a few years, I was happier than I'd ever been in my young life. And the prestige I commanded among the small community of physicians and nurses was heady stuff for a young woman in her early twenties. The girl from the east coast had become something of a celebrity at St. Luke's Hospital in Houston, Texas. I loved working with the physicians and seriously considered an offer to work with the Cardiology group to come on full-time with them to function as a physician's assistant. These were exciting times in cardiovascular surgery and medicine. The first mechanical heart transplant, 'firsts' of all types were accumulating in Houston, and I was tempted. But late one evening right before I got married while I was still considering the offer, I went over to the head cardiologist's office. Just as I was about to knock , then open the door, I realized that he was not alone, one of the senior surgeons was with him. They were arguing about a patient who had been transferred from somewhere in the Midwest. The cardiologist was arguing because the man's coronary arteries were clean, meaning free of blockage. Then I heard the surgeon say firmly, "Bob, he flew here for a bypass, we're going to give him a bypass." More than a little of the passion I felt in working with these men eroded that night.

I got married because I quite literally did not know what else to do. We moved to Detroit the day after we got married because my new husband had a new job there. Like me, he was ambitious, but for money. My husband's world was a practical one, very like my mother's. Discussing ideas and philosophies were of no interest to him. Many people tried to talk me out of the marriage because it was evident to anyone who knew me that my husband and I had too little in common. My Dad, more than anyone, pointed out the polar nature of our interests and goals. But my mind was closed, I was incapable of listening.

Only when I became pregnant during our first year of marriage did I begin to realize the dreadful consequences of all the lies I had told myself. Lies such as never wanting to marry or never wanting to have children. In a desperate war with myself, I was incapable of a mature relationship. The marriage was unfair to my husband from the beginning. How could he understand my feelings when the Obstetrician I had picked out of the yellow pages confirmed my fear that the IUD he had inserted six weeks before had failed?. When I couldn't or wouldn't express them? I was pregnant. The awe, wonder, amazement of it. Despite the adultery and pre-marital sex, I was able to conceive this child I claimed I did not want. Conflicting emotions rocked me to the core. So powerful that I could not handle them, and I knew no one to whom I could talk about the fact that I felt completely trapped. I had the abortion because I felt I had no choice. My husband had met and married a young woman who claimed no interest in children, one committed to her career, sharply opposed to the woman he left to marry me, the mother of his two boys. He had two young children and had been delighted when I claimed I never wanted kids. I was well aware of how persuasive I had been because I'd convinced myself.

Both he and I ignored the fact that my clothes were getting tighter while my body changed dramatically, it seemed, by the minute. There was no doubt that what I knew I had to do was murder, the euphemism fetus, and its attendant claims that these were not babies but some prehuman entity had not yet taken root. With whom do you talk when you believe you have to kill your baby? I attempted once to speak with a psychiatric nurse specialist at the hospital where I worked. She was kind and very caring. Mostly, though, she gently tried to persuade me that I was making the decision much harder by my insistence on using the word murder. It was an abortion, after all, not murder. And once I called a dear friend who listened then told me that my reaction was normal, everything would change once I had the baby.

But I knew I could not have that baby.

I waited until it was almost too late for the abortion. Only the night before I left for the flight to New York, did my husband and I finally discuss what was happening. At his suggestion that we go out to dinner to talk about it, I completely lost control, screaming and hollering that there was no way I could eat since I was preparing to commit murder. He had never seen me like this and had no idea of how to react. Of course, he didn't, he had quite naturally believed what I had told him. My husband never had any inkling of the anguish I was experiencing since I never voiced any of this.

Looking back on those painful days, I wonder what would have happened had I opened my heart to the wisdom and counsel of my mother, sisters, or friends with children. But I believed that if I gave birth to Nicole, (I named her during those weeks of pretending she was not there) that I would be condemning myself to live the life that had trapped my mother and sisters. And I would be as imprisoned as they seemed to be. I convinced myself that my promise to my husband that we would remain childless took precedence over doing what I knew was right. And used silly 'logical' arguments like it would be 'wrong' to bring a child into the world who was not wanted by both her parents.

In 1973, the only place for a legal abortion was in New York City. I stayed at the apartment of one of the friends who had been with me that Easter Sunday, that Easter Sunday that I'd realized I had lost my faith. My friend was worried. She could see the unhealthy ways I was dealing with all of this. Jeanne knew and liked my husband and was rightly concerned about whether our marriage could survive this. Trying to console me, confiding that she had gone to the same hospital for an abortion two years before, she talked into the night that long weekend. But I could not hear her. I was married, not single like her. Somehow aborting a baby seemed far less terrible for a single woman than for a married one.

Many decades after my college friend Kathy created and framed her beautifully scripted "Four Stumbling Blocks To Truth," it remains prominently displayed in my home office. Kathy and I were close in the way of very young women with remarkable commonalities. Both of us had walked away from our respective faiths, Kathy had been Catholic. Just like me, she had walked away from religion, from God. Each of us had moved far away, she from New York and I from Massachusetts. And both of us were intensely ambitious, gifted, and terrified about the presence of our particular gifts. About what they meant and what we should do with them. A few months before I turned down the Fordham University scholarship, Kathy refused a full tuition scholarship to study art in Florence.

Both of us worked in the Cooley ICU while putting ourselves through Dominican College. The irony of the Catholicity of the College was lost on neither of us. We had lengthy, passionate discussions about the meaning of life, about truth, about death, about being young, ambitious and female. Often we would talk long into the night. When one of our professors at the college mentioned Sandburg's listing we memorized it, agreeing that these were a recipe for us to guide our lives, attributing authorship to atheist Sandburg. Oblivious to the fact that the four maxims had been formulated centuries before Sandburg by a Catholic Monk. Roger Bacon, a thirteenth-century monk, had created the obstacles to truth: the influence of fragile and unworthy authority, custom, the imperfection of undisciplined senses and concealment of ignorance by ostentation of wisdom. I cried the night Kathy gave me the framed beautifully calligraphed words which served as the rules by which I wanted to live my life. It was my graduation present. Unmentioned by the philosopher in his weighty profound list of obstacles to truth is the most important of all. The need to be truthful to self, the extraordinary harm we do to ourselves and others when we believe our own lies.

CHAPTER FIVE

A Lost Marriage

AFTER THE ABORTION, I did the only thing I knew to do. I went on with my life and pretended that I had never been pregnant. Or that I knew she had been a girl whom I had secretly named Nicole. My husband and I talked about the baby only twice, the night before I was to fly to Manhattan for the abortion and a couple of years later when he bought a Doberman puppy for my birthday. In an attempt to replace the child who never had a chance at life.

I was successful at suppressing the memory of what I'd done because of the business of our lives. My husband was successfully pursuing his career and moving up quickly in the medical sales company he worked for. His schedule of very long hours and traveling extensively for his job left me with lots of time alone in a city where I knew no one.

But my Houston experience was invaluable in the eyes of Detroit Hospitals, and I quickly landed jobs for which I should have had an advanced degree. Aware that I needed a master's to continue the teaching and supervisory work I had learned to love in the still new specialty of critical care, I did well enough in a bachelor's in nursing equivalency battery of tests for acceptance into the Masters of Nursing Program at Wayne State University.

But just before the start of my first semester in graduate school, my husband received another promotion, and we moved to Boston. The Wayne State acceptance transferred quickly to Boston University where I received a Master of Science in nursing. Immediately following graduation, I landed a job at the prestigious Massachusetts General Hospital but for just six months for we moved once again. In ten years of marriage, we moved seven times.

It was in Boston where I first encountered feminists, many radically so. The most hard-hitting was a woman with a doctorate in Theology, a professor at the Catholic Boston College, who fostered a strident campaign for women to become priests. She was articulate and aggressive therefore obtained extensive print and television coverage. It was the seventies, fertile ground for extremism from all directions.

I was not Catholic, had no interest in Catholicism or any religion for that matter. But what struck me most forcefully was her anger, actually, rage, at priests, at men. And when she spoke, she used the vocabulary of power and politics. I thought it strange that she hardly mentioned God. I became curious and read several books by feminists. Once again, much of the content was about power: men had it, and women needed to grab it. There was something off in the thinking; I could not relate nor make sense of most of the arguments. These people seemed angry, not all, but the majority of the authors I read. And the anger was targeted at men.

So I mentally discarded the whole notion of feminism, thinking I had nothing in common with these women. During one of the very few conversations we had on the subject, my husband casually commented about a woman we both knew, 'she seems like a feminist, like you.' Startled, I asked him if he actually thought that. He looked at me and merely asked wearily, "You don't think you both are waging some kind of war?"

I said nothing. Because he was terribly right. I was waging some war and had been for too many years. But it wasn't at men. Or at my husband although I most likely acted that way. My battle was unwinnable because I had no clue who the combatants were. Or how to find out.

True enough that when people began saying that I 'argued like a man' or 'drove like a man' that I took it as the highest form of flattery. Also true that my mother was classically female in that she seemed to let her emotions rule her thoughts and opinions. When we spoke about ideas or principles at home, my mother was unapologetic when expressing her highly emotional basis for her beliefs. She seemed illogical, even irrational to me and I was embarrassed for her. The lack of logic indicated a lack of intelligence. Convinced that neither my mother or most of my female friends could understand my ambition and desire to 'do something' with my life, I kept it all bottled up inside. Rather than being angry at men, I liked them, even preferring male friendships to female. It seemed to me that I could understand men better than women.

I was working closely with cardiac residents, attendings, anesthesiologists, mostly men and with critical care nurses, mostly women. But they were smart and tough, and I liked the work. After Boston came Hartford where the Associate Director of Cardiac Surgery was a surgeon I had known in Houston. It was like old home week when we saw one another in the cardiac ICU. Although I had dreaded leaving the job in Boston at Mass General, this new one felt even better to me. By now, I made professional friendships quickly and became accustomed to living alone while my husband traveled three weeks out of four. A couple of the nurses at my level were single and, like me enjoyed the symphony and plays.

Despite my internal chaos, each geographic move resulted in better jobs for us both. My husband and I lived parallel lives, working long days and often the weekends. The work of recreating myself in each new city proved to be excellent for my self-confidence and ability to become quickly well- known in my field.

After only six months in Tulsa, I was seriously considered for a senior executive position at one of the private hospitals. I became excited about the prospect of moving into senior management. After successfully interviewing as one of a dozen candidates for the position, I received high praise from insiders close to the CEO of the hospital.

But then the insomnia hit. Not a mere few sleepless nights but weeks which stretched into months of no sleep. Although I was barely thirty-two, I began to suspect cardiac problems and sought out a complete cardiac workout because of the chest pains I experienced during those endless nights from one of the docs with whom I had worked and respected.

After a full workup, the internist pronounced me healthy and attributed the sleeplessness to stress. He prescribed sleeping pills and suggested that I withdraw from the chief nursing job explaining that the last thing I needed was more stress. But neither the pills nor pulling back on my work hours helped. Even drastic measures like moving into the guest bedroom, ear plugs, sleeping pills along with the use of multiple fans as white noise did not stop the nightly routine of dread. Exhausted, I would finally give in to the fatigue and assemble all my pharmaceutical and mechanical aids to sleep. But just as I was about to drop into sleep, I would start, sometimes violently, and lie awake until exhaustion once again tried to pull me into sleep only to startle awake. It was, in a word, hell. Only many years later did I learn that I was manifesting most of the typical signs of a woman who had an abortion and never dealt with the aftermath.

When his suggestions to see a psychiatrist and then later a divorce went unanswered, my husband asked in quasi-desperation if I thought moving back to Houston may help. I jumped on his proposal. Within a few weeks, we were moving to Texas and buying a house in the suburbs to the north of the city.

The return to Houston helped, for a while. My insomnia ended as quickly as it had begun and I was delighted to be back in Texas. For very few months, I worked at Ben Taub Hospital, the county hospital in Houston. The hospital I wanted had no openings in management, and I had never before worked in a public hospital. I was one of maybe five Caucasians working in the hospital system; patients and staff were African-American, and I got an excellent introduction to the profound impact of looking perfectly opposite from everyone else.

It was during those few months where I was first introduced to the startling notion of health by a friend who was currently working on her doctorate in Public Health. I had been working in critical care for close to fifteen years and never had considered the concept. What it meant. And the chasm between medicine and health. My friend worked in the education department for the county and invited me to a three-day conference on holistic health. From the first speaker, I was riveted.

The opening presenter was a trial attorney. He could move only his lips and facial muscles and was a captivating speaker. Without a trace of bitterness or rancor, he told of the vast ignorance about health in the medical profession. He had severed his spinal cord in a diving accident at eighteen and was told by his doctors that he needed to forget his dreams of law school and accept that he would never be able to go to college or have children, and would be dependent on machines for the rest of his life. The entire conference was exhilarating and exciting and felt right. Excited, I told my husband about the meeting when he got home from a trip.

After I finally wound down, my ever practical husband asked if there was a way I could apply all my knowledge and passion and come up with a way to make money. More than any other move in the years we had been married, this one had been mostly for me, in hopes that our marriage could be salvaged. Unspoken but we both understood the implicit understanding.

Since I had already started up the management track and had an impressive resume, once a job opened up at Hermann Hospital, I was selected from a sizeable group of internal and external candidates for Director of Medical Nursing. I ending up working there for almost twenty years. The job was challenging, I was delighted to be back in the Texas Medical Center and liked the people I worked with, one of whom was one of four editors for a successful Critical Care Nursing Textbook. My writing was also beginning to bring me some acclaim in the field of critical care nursing.

Therefore, when an editor from Blackwell Scientific Publications called to ask me to write a cardiovascular textbook, I was flattered, excited and instantly agreed to his offer. Another writer friend advised me against asking others to join me as an editor. Cornelia said that the negotiations with her three colleagues had been a nightmare from the beginning of their text. The four could agree on nothing, even the most trivial details. Therefore, she advised me to be the sole editor for my book.

I never gave *any* thought to how I would assemble the number of contributing authors needed for the comprehensive text I envisioned. Nor did I take the time to consider just where I would find the time to get this done. This was the very early Eighties when writing and publishing were wholly different industries. There was no internet; all communication had to be done by mail and telephone. Research was possible only through the traditional methods of libraries and purchase of the source books. Working full-time with a new and demanding job and a husband, I could work on the book only during weekends and vacations. I justified my decision with the fact that my husband still traveled most of the time, and we continued to live the parallel lives we'd been living for years.

On occasion, during her yearly visits, my mother would state the obvious, in her attempts to help save the marriage she saw eroding in front of her eyes. She had grown to love and respect my husband and feared for our relationship. Mom could not understand why I had taken on such an immense project like the textbook and wished I would be a wife rather than this career person who made no sense to her. And I could not understand why she refused to share my excitement about the progress I was making in my career. When I think back on those few conversations, I feel mostly sadness. It seemed as if we each stood on either side of an abyss, exclaiming incomprehensible words to one another.

The book was the final straw for my husband, understandably so. We were unhappily married. It was apparent to both of us that we were happier alone or in the company of friends, but we were never able to speak about what the problems were. Sexually, there had been problems for years. Problems that required professional help, in retrospect. The textbook was published two years after our divorce was final.

By the time I did see a psychiatrist, it was too late for the marriage. I had come apart when we split because the reality of my total failure in marriage had overwhelmed me. At the suggestion of my worried sister, I went to talk with her priest at the Episcopalian Church where she and her family attended services in north Houston.

I did go to see the priest several times. Initially, I kept our discussions to the superficial, unsure of why I was there, talking with this man. Over a few meetings with me, he gently asked questions which required more than yes or no answers. And was generous enough to come to the hospital for our meetings. It was patently evident to him that there was a deeper reason for my sadness, beyond the divorce, one that I was unaware of.

At our last meeting in the cafeteria of the hospital, it all came back, like a tidal wave of horror. What I had done all those years ago and the now defunct marriage for which I had done it. Nicole, the baby, the abortion in New York. I began to sob right there in the cafeteria. Quietly, Clark suggested we go somewhere private and continued in my office for a long time. Very lovingly, he listened, asking no questions until finally, I stopped. Unexpectantly, Clarke began to pray and gave me absolution. Saying, as he did so that God understood why I had done what I had. And forgave me.

I do not remember the words he used during the prayer because of the powerful light that appeared suddenly in my office, filling it. I kept asking Clark why he could not see the bright light which shone so brightly over our heads that I had to squint at him to see him. That light followed us as I walked him to his car, thankful for his loving concern. I asked again if he didn't see that light, pointing up at it. But he could not. Only much later, after I saw that same light a third time did I figure out I had seen the Holy Spirit.

Shrugging off my claims about the strange light, the priest suggested I seek professional help. He had heard enough in the four or five conversations we'd had to think therapy would help. Clarke suggested I see his friend Jamie, " A Baylor-trained psychiatrist, you'll like her Lin, and she'll like you." True, we did. I saw Jamie for over a year, my ex-husband insisting on paying for the costly weekly visits.

When my husband and I finally let one another go, I encountered that familiar anger that some women hold for men once again. My friends and family, without exception, were entirely on 'my side', placing me as the victim and him as my tormentor. That my husband and I had hired the same lawyer was pure idiocy in the minds of these women with whom I had become very close very quickly. Most everyone was sure that he had been cheating on me as he had on his first wife with me. And were baffled when I replied that I did not blame him. I did not know if he had been seeing someone else. Most likely he had been, but I meant it when I said what I did because it really made no difference in the end.

The truth, the reality of the entire ten years was simple. I had no business marrying my husband, knew nothing about love or being a wife and never bothered to learn. Worse yet, I'd been utterly confused about who and what I was, presenting myself as a knowledgeable, committed career woman, sure of her goals. In fact, the only purpose I had certainty about was a negative one, I wanted to live a life entirely different from that of my mother. When the marriage was finally over, I felt sad at the failure, regret at the cost but also an enormous relief. I had been afraid of being alone and realized that feeling alone in a marriage is far lonelier than living alone.

CHAPTER SIX

Career: More School and More Work

THE DAY THEY VOTED ME in as the new chair of the Institutional Ethics Committee for Hermann Hospital, I enrolled at University of Texas School of Public Health to start work on my doctorate. The technologic innovations developed within critical care over the last twenty years had created a brand new problem within medicine. It was becoming difficult to die in hospitals here in the US and in much of the Western world. Life-saving techniques and equipment were used for all patients. For all too many, the new therapies merely extended the process of dying, causing the families as well as the patients great suffering and exorbitant costs. Patients who were riddled with cancer, multiple system failures or people with devastating brain injuries were maintained by the ventilator or artificial breathing machine.

The problem was a simple one but the solution far less so. How and when do we withdraw lifesaving technology? Even more fundamentally, how do we define which therapies to stop and who should make the decision to stop? What exactly do we mean by death when we can artificially breathe and chemically manipulate the heart? Doctors were in the business of saving lives, not helping people die.

Perhaps the hardest thing for any of us to do is nothing. To hold back when we have relevant knowledge which can clarify, even resolve a problem or save a life. But in medicine, fighting the use of life-saving techniques we know as well as the palm of our hand can be torture. I remember clearly watching a patient die when I could easily have shocked his heart back into normal rhythm and mediated the irritability in his heart with an intravenous medication. But he was a DNR. I remember still his name, Victor Ortiz. I was a very young nurse working in the Cardiac ICU in New York City and stood helplessly while his monitor showed easily treatable arrhythmias. After multiple surgical procedures, the medical staff had determined that there was nothing more that could be done. So I stood staring at his monitor, watching the electrical signals slowly lose amplitude until finally there was merely a straight line.

In 1985, the increasing numbers of these kinds of patients were off in a corner of an intensive care unit or hospital floor attended primarily by nurses. When their hearts stopped working efficiently, or they stopped breathing, standard hospital practice was to restart the heart and breathing either manually or more commonly with drugs and machines. Nurses were instructed to 'call a code' and much of the time, the patient was revived enough to be transferred back to the ICU where the whole cycle could begin again. In a teaching hospital where there were resident doctors available twenty-four hours a day, seven days a week, codes were a highlight for the interns and residents, exciting opportunities to practice bringing people back to life. With the help of two private doctors, I wrote a policy listing the criteria for which patients would not be resuscitated called a DNR. And we listed additional treatments like dialysis and pharmaceutical aids to blood pressure and cardiac function in a category we called extraordinary measures therefore appropriate to be withheld in a patient classified as DNR. Then we three did round the clock classes for medical students, residents, and attendings about the situations where it was morally best to withhold resuscitation. The DNR is an anomaly in the extensive vocabulary of doctors orders in that this was a medical order to not treat. Because of my extensive work with the subject, the Hospital Chaplain, who began the Ethics Committee asked for my help and had invited me to join a year earlier.

I was sitting in the office of the Chairman of Pediatrics at the University of Texas Medical School. We were talking about the fact that the Chaplain Chair of our ethics committee had resigned from the hospital.

"Who are you thinking for Chair?" I asked innocently.

"We had a meeting of the physician members of the committee last night. We elected you."

Stunned, I sat staring into his dark blue twinkling eyes, speechless. We were an academic medical center, I had assumed that the new Chairman would be one of the department chairs, even him.

"Jan, I cannot even spell ethics! I know nothing about how to run an ethics committee!

Jan Van Eys was an authentic gentleman and a scholar, full of wisdom, and I respected the man deeply. His dark blue eyes gazed at me, unfazed at my discomfort and fumbling. Then after a moment, he nodded and said, "Yes, that is exactly why we want you, you'll do no harm."

I laughed. A back-handed compliment to be sure but I knew what he meant.

This was perfect. I felt honored at the trust the doctors had in me. Also, this was a huge problem, one that was causing misery in so many lives. And one I could do something about, maybe even fix.

I had been thinking about a doctorate but had not been able to make up my mind. In fact, my current boss was pushing hard for me to go back to school. But I had been reluctant for a couple of reasons. The last degree, the Master's at Boston University had been disappointing and extremely expensive. It had been mostly perfunctory, a way to provide a 'ticket' of the letters after my name because masters degrees had become the norm. If I went back for a doctorate, I needed the process to be challenging and purposeful. I wanted to be changed by the process. The few times I made the mistake of saying this to my associates, they laughed. Too idealistic.

Just as critical in my decision was whether I could get up the stamina to go back to school. The textbook had taken far more than I had bargained for, six years of work and pressure. A doctorate would easily take six years, probably more because I worked a full-time job. So once again, I'd be sacrificing weekends and vacations for an untold number of years. Would a doctorate be worth it?

But with this decision of the docs at my hospital, the decision was made for me. I would do my dissertation on whether medical decision making in the terminally ill could be helped by Institutional Ethics Committees. I had a plan once again.

Like many of my physician colleagues, I believed death an enemy and suffering pointless if not evil. Where there was pain, our job was to alleviate it, and where there were no more medical miracles to apply, we needed to help the person die with dignity. Even if it meant hastening death with opiates, the suffering must be stopped. I chaired the ethics committee at Hermann for over ten years. The Chaplain had laid the groundwork for me by following the guidelines of the Ethics Committee at Mass General, the first in the country to establish an IEC. Most of the policies and guidelines were in place.

We began hearing cases a couple of months after I took over as Chair. Perhaps because I was a nurse with the background in critical care, the first few cases were merely a matter of the committee rubber stamping what the attending physician knew needed to be done. The state of Texas had passed natural death legislation where an individual could direct medical personnel to withhold live saving measures, but the wording of the act was ambiguous, necessarily. The medical staff requested formal backup from the committee, legal backup in a word as they took a patient off the ventilator or stopped dialysis. Because the fear of lawsuits is so predominant in the minds of doctors, the presence of a lawyer on the committee was critical.

Like many complex subjects, medical ethics is a collection of disciplines. By the time I had completed my doctorate and had chaired the Committee for close to ten years, I was called an 'expert' in medical ethics. But I had come to view ethics as an amalgamation of the law, morality, and the social sciences rather than its own discipline.

I became friends with the General Counsel for the hospital because he helped me out of the huge jam with the publisher for my textbook. Finally, I had all forty-five chapters done. Except for the one titled 'Legalities of Critical Care'. The contributor responsible for that chapter had not only been way behind the deadline he had agreed to but submitted a substandard paper. It was disorganized, almost incoherent.

I did not know Randy, General Counsel for Hermann Hospital but reckoned there could be only two replies to my request when I knocked on his office door and asked to speak to him about a personal problem. After Randy most agreeably said sure, he could write the chapter for me, he smiled and asked when I needed it. The smile broadened when I replied that I needed to get it in the mail to the publisher that next weekend. Four days from the day we spoke. In two days, he had his assistant deliver it to my office. The content was far superior to that of the original contributor, and I was exceedingly grateful.

Because of our work on the committee, we began to work closely together. And found that we each had an ability to drill down into the details of the case so that the issues could be identified. Often, the doctor knew that the patient should be taken off the ventilator but merely needed institutional authority to back him up. Once the IEC began using the form Randy had developed, the medical staff felt support in their decisions.

When we suggested the use of pain relievers once the ventilator was removed, many of the doctors were relieved to know they could do this. Watching an individual fight for breath can be a terrible thing to witness. Word spread through the medical staff, and we were soon hearing two to three cases a week.

Not long after I became Chair of the Hermann Ethics Committee, my family was faced with withdrawing the ventilator from my mother at an outlying hospital in Houston. Fourteen years before, my barely sixty-year-old mother was diagnosed with atherosclerosis and high blood pressure. Mom construed these two diagnoses as a death sentence and developed what her Florida cardiologist admitted was 'morbid anxiety' but claimed he could do nothing about it when I insisted on accompanying my father for a meeting with her doctor.

Obediently quitting smoking for a time, my mother gained weight she could never lose even when she returned to smoking. Refusing to do any type of exercise because she claimed her legs hurt when she walked, her weight skyrocketed. While she did little other than sit on her couch and smoke.

Time after time, while visiting her and my father in Florida where they had retired, I would try to explain that neither of these two conditions was life-threatening. Even drawing pictures of the heart along with the one-way valves in the leg veins to help her see how important walking alternately annoyed or amused her.

Long before I had my doctorate, she would call me Dr. Lin during these frustrating conversations. She was happiest only when admitted to the hospital when her angina frightened her so badly that Dad would take here to the emergency room.

The winter she died, my parents had come to Houston for Christmas, staying first with me where my mother caught my cold and then with my sister Lee who decided to take Mom to the hospital where she worked as a nurse. Within a couple of hours, the emergency medicine docs had her on a ventilator and transferred her to intensive care. By the time I got out to see her that night, she had been resuscitated twice.

Through the fourteen years during which my mother lived as a cardiac cripple, she would beg all of us, Dad and my two sisters, to promise that we would not allow her to end up comatose and on machines to keep her vital functions going. That night, when I got to her bedside, it was all too clear to me that she was exactly where she had feared to be. A crisis like this tears at families and ours was no different. There were huge aliquots of grief, blame, and guilt distributed among the four of us.

That night the attending physician agreed to write a DNR order for Mom, meaning that if her heart were to stop again, she would be given no resuscitative drugs or procedures. But her heart never stopped. In fact, when her doctors finally agreed to let me see her tests, her electrocardiograms showed no sign of infarct or even ischemia. Despite the fifteen years, Mom had lived as a cardiac cripple, her heart was perfectly healthy.

As the days wore on with no change, Mother's attending physician agreed to a neurological consult. The neurologist believed she was in a persistent vegetative state due to severe oxygen lack, sustained during the two arrests. My family finally agreed with me that we needed to respect Mom's wishes and invoke the legislation which had been passed precisely for these particular circumstances. In the mid-Eighties, few doctors had even heard of the Texas Natural Death Act. I was well aware that this would be horrendously difficult for Mom's attending physician who I knew would prefer to deal with his living patients and ignore this whole tragic scenario. But after ten years of watching my mother head inexorably toward death, incapable of taking one step toward her own health, I was single-minded. This was one thing we could protect her from. Ending up in a nursing home with no cognitive faculties, the end which so horrified her. Another deep regret was that I did not stay in her room after the ventilator was removed. I could have stayed there, talking with her and praying out loud with her had I known how to pray. Instead, I walked away.

CHAPTER SEVEN

Hitting the Wall

BY THE TIME THAT then New York Times reporter Lisa Belkin showed up to write her first book, *First Do No Harm*, about our committee, Randy, the hospital lawyer and I were living together. Lisa and I frequently joked about which would come first, her book or my doctorate through the two years she observed the patients and families who were brought to the committee. Her book came first, by two years.

"Come see me, Lin."

I had just finished a presentation at the School of Public Health about the results of my study, the data from my dissertation. The applause had been fairly unanimous, none of the questions tough and the audience seemed impressed by my talk and about what the Ethics Committee was doing down the street at Hermann Hospital.

As I collected my materials and began to leave, Steve Linder, came close enough for him to quietly ask, "How are you doing?"

At my, "Awful, awful, awful," reply and the sudden sting of embarrassing tears in my eyes, my former dissertation chair and advisor nodded. Steve seemed unsurprised.

I had graduated from school, seven years of classes, preparation for qualifying examinations, and two years of working with my dissertation committee. Finally, the defense of my paper. It was done. People now called me Doctor and treated me with a new deference and respect. And I wondered why.

Lisa Belkin's book had been translated into numerous languages, and Hollywood was considering a movie based on her book, *First Do No Harm*. The Australian screenwriter they had hired for the film, had flown out from Hollywood to Houston to shadow Randy and me. Robert had completed the screenplay, he merely wanted to 'dress it up.' Part of the attraction of many a film was the romantic interest between leading characters. Since the chair of the committee and its lawyer were romantically involved, the screenwriter wanted to get to know us both. To put flesh and bones on the characters based on Randy and me, Robert explained.

A most down-to-earth and gracious man, Robert Caswell was generous enough to talk extensively with me about how he had created the screenplay for the film, *The Doctor*. For many years, I kept the page with the circular outline he had drawn when I asked how he had created the story. When I confessed my dreams of writing fiction someday, Robert used smaller and smaller circles to explain how he conceived his story about a transformation of an arrogant, obnoxious surgeon to a human being. The writer had spent a couple of hours clarifying that everything radiated from the main character's sudden diagnosis of cancer. That was the critical event in the life of the main character, therefore, the center dot of the circle, all other elements of the story radiating about the central event. Incredibly heady stuff.

I had so many offers to speak and consult with academic health centers around the country about ethics and management that I could not accept them all, just did not have the time. I had achieved all the dreams that I told my mother I wanted to, I had 'done something with my life.' In many circles, I was known and in some, 'famous.' And I had never been more miserable.

During the two years, while I worked on my dissertation evenings, weekends and vacations, the Hermann Hospital administration continued its frequent administrative shake-ups. For some inexplicable reason, I was not one of the many mid-level long-term people laid off but was instead brought back into operations several months before another massive shake-up. This one took out the entire senior administration almost overnight.

The new Chief Executive Officer had been a breath of fresh air. Harry and I liked one another from the moment we met. With his deceptively simple philosophy where administrators were to stay out of the way of expert physicians and nurses, the climate of the entire institution changed from one of fear to excitement. Harry was a joy to work with. I was now a Senior Vice-President, one of four of us running a nine-hundred-bed hospital. For two years, I worked harder than I ever had in my life but loved every minute of it.

Excited, I stopped in his office at six-thirty on the morning of the day of my dissertation defense, mostly to tease my boss, let him know that I would expect to be called 'Doctor" after eleven that morning. There were boxes everywhere. Stunned, I merely stood in the door of his office and stared, dumbfounded. Harry stopped packing for a moment to shrug and tell me that the Board had fired him the night before. And that I shouldn't be talking to him, the Board had given him just an hour to be out.

Within days, the upset made national news. The man who had turned around a failing teaching hospital, close to bankruptcy, had been summarily fired by the Board of Trustees of Hermann Hospital. That night, at home, Randy told me to stay away from Harry, he had broken the law and might be subject to federal indictments for financially incentivizing doctors to practice at the hospital. To my shame, I listened to him. I never called Harry to tell him how sorry I was for what had happened. To let him know how much I had loved working for him.

When I did get to Steve's office to talk as he had requested, I asked him how he had known to even ask the question never mind take the time to talk. We spoke for a long time, probably close to two hours, maybe more. I confessed to him that I had sat, alone on the steps of the school, sobbing after I passed my qualifying exams. I did not tell Steve that Randy had passed from worry through concern and was heading rapidly toward disinterest. Once I refused his suggestion of seeing a psychiatrist, he began to withdraw emotionally. Many times, he shook his head in frustration at my depression. His word, not mine. Since all he had wanted to do was celebrate after passing the Bar, he had assumed that we would be 'back to normal' once school was over. Even worse than my abnormal response to a significant achievement was my inability to explain why I felt the way I did, to him or to anyone. The closeness we had had for years was evaporating, and all I could do was watch passively.

But to my stunned surprise, I felt understood rather than embarrassed when Steve and I talked. Most likely, though, it was I who talked and Steve who listened to my pent up emotions. All of them beginning with this feeling of extreme unease and embarrassment. Embarrassed because to the casual observer, I was living the perfect life. Randy and I were called 'the Golden couple' both blonde and attractive. The aura surrounding us was even brighter because of the possibility of a movie, partially based on us. We were seen as 'movers and shakers' in the medical center and within the hospital, I was a very powerful individual. During the last administrative shakeup, Harry had taken me from middle management to a position of real authority. Because of my budgetary power over large medical departments, a couple of the Faculty Department Chairs were ingratiating in their manner around me. It was comical, but I couldn't laugh. It all felt fake. And most of what I did on a daily basis seemed like gamesmanship, void of any meaning. Once Harry had been fired, all of the passion for what I did had died. Overnight. The people I worked with were decent people, to be sure, but they lacked the fire, the passion that Harry Neer had. I realized that I hated what I did.

"Because you have been living in the world of the intellectual for seven years. Because this is where you derive your passion, not in the boardrooms or the politics of power. I knew you would have a tough re-entry into your world, now that you've no relief from it." Steve smiled, "Welcome to the world of the intellectual, Lin." He paused reflectively while he thought about what to say next. "You'll find that all these people you have studied over the years will feel like friends when you encounter them again. But the actual work, the day- to- day is just work, no matter where we do it, we cannot escape the games, the politics. It's where a lot of people live." He must have read my mind because I wondered if it would be any better in academia. Clearly, it would not be.

"Why is it that by the time I finally have the credentials to join a club, I am no longer interested in belonging to it?"

There was no answer to my question, but one thing was sure. I had loved all the years of hard work and study for the doctorate. I had no regrets and was proud of having the degree. But I'd finally figured out that all the initials after my name, titles, and big salaries did not create the contentment, sense of accomplishment, the peace I had hoped for. It was time to look elsewhere.

CHAPTER EIGHT

Greece, Alone

I WAS NOT ALL that surprised when Randy told me he was leaving. Hurt, disappointed, sorrowful but not surprised. He had not been happy for a couple of years and had said so. Early in our relationship, he had suggested that we explore Catholicism together, perhaps even become Catholic. A highly spiritual person, Randy had considered the ministry in his teens but was talked out of it by his family. We had relished our conversations about all things mystical and unworldly. But I was still too focused on career goals to undertake another commitment, specifically a religious one.

Randy's unhappiness was understandable because, for years, my list of priorities placed him after school and work. That had been so for the entire seven years I had been in school. At great length, we had discussed the commitment going for the doctorate would entail before I enrolled. But after a few years, the grind got to him- he had worked his way through law school, after all, passed the bar and was done. He had no interest in returning to the world of academics. After work, he merely wanted to kick back, have fun. And many weekends, he took off with a friend and did not come back until late Sunday night. Patterns tend not to change, neither my own or that of the men I was attracted to. I knew he was married when we met, how could I be surprised if he had found someone else with more time for him?

Because we were both in senior administration at the hospital, our offices merely fifty feet from one another, our breakup was hardly private. Despite our attempts to maintain our professional cool, meetings, social functions, even casual encounters in the hallway became intolerable for me. I knew I needed to leave the hospital and Texas as quickly as possible and began to seek out jobs in other parts of the country. Soon, I was contacted by a search firm looking for a Hospital Director at a teaching hospital in Massachusetts. They wanted someone with a nursing background, and I had met both the Financial Officer and Director of Nursing at meetings. Perhaps this could work so I began the process of interviewing for the job. After the initial round of interviews, I learned that I was on the short list, meaning that I'd made the cuts down to a list of three, me and two others. The decision would be made in late summer or early fall.

Randy and I had been planning a trip to Greece with close friends for over a year that last summer I spent in Houston. Actually, the idea of going to Greece had been suggested by our friends. Two years before, the four of us had traveled to Paris and northern France and found the trip to be more than special. Perhaps, Greece was an attempt to recreate those idyllic ten days. Once our friend Jamie brought up the idea of Greece, memories sparked in me: Plato, Socrates, Delphi, the glory of ancient Greece, I was hooked.

Randy and I and our two friends had even been for dinner at the home of one of the neuroscientists at the medical school whom I worked with. We had become friendly during some business travel. On the flight back to Houston from the University we had visited together, Andy was just making conversation when he asked, 'Do you like what you do'? Both of us noticed that it was a simple 'yes' or 'no' question that I could not answer. Rather, I stammered and floundered then finally changed the subject, hoping he would not notice my evasiveness.

    Dr. Andy Papalicanou is wholly Greek, clear about where his real home is and the tradeoffs for not living there. He loves his country and its people with a passion, explaining to the four of us that night at dinner that the sole reason he lived in Houston was work. All Americans know how to do, he had said wistfully is to work and make money. And all that Greeks knew how to do is live and love. They neither know nor care about work or money.

    Andy's eyes lit up that evening while he talked with us about his native land and places he suggested we not miss. Places like the 'rock that Zeus split' in Delphi. Delphi...even the name connoted wisdom, rare and esoteric. I decided to go. Alone.

    The first round of interviews had gone very well at the Massachusetts job. But I knew there were over nine other candidates for the position. The next step would be to pare down the ten of us to a 'shortlist' of three. I had felt very comfortable during the interviews and felt confident that I would return for the next set. But I also suspected there were could be a huge benefit if I got out of town, way outside the city. There was little I could do other than wait while the people at the place I hoped to work made up their minds. And everywhere I looked, it seemed, I saw pity in people's eyes. I had loved living in Texas, had come to love everything about the crazy place and its sometimes redneck citizens, but I knew I needed to leave.

    I had never traveled by myself. But inside all the sorrow, loss, and so many conflicting emotions was a sense that if I got away, way away, I might find what I could not even name. A country which spoke a language comprised of letters I could not understand seemed perfect.

But I needed some help to set up the trip. And the only Greek I knew well enough to ask for help was Andy. When I got to his office that June day, I was nervous, uncomfortable and initially wondering what I was doing there. After all, I hardly knew this guy but finally blurted out that I guessed he had heard about Randy and me. Quickly at his somber nod, before he could say anything else, I told him I wanted to go on the trip we planned, alone. Because...Andy leaned over and gently touched my arm to say, "Because you need to go somewhere you have never been. You need to experience sights you have never seen, you need to heal." Those were most assuredly not his exact words but were close enough.

"I'm leaving in three weeks because one of my students is defending his dissertation at the University of Crete. I am flying into Athens; I'll make the arrangements if you can make the same ten-day trip. And I'll also get you some reservations near Nafplio, one of my favorite cities, Talos is a beach town near there. Perfect for you. Can you come?"

Oh, could I, yes, indeed. There were a few more details to be discussed but by the first week in July, I sat listening to five maybe six of Andy's Greek friends talk long into the night during a dinner on the island of Crete. I loved it. Andy had warned me that Greek dinners begin at ten and end around two in the morning, maybe. I was the only woman, spoke no Greek and felt more at home than I had in I could not recall when. The air was balmy, the food simple but delicious. And I understood what they talked about only through their gestures and body language. It was wonderful.

Occasionally one of the men would notice my silent presence and whisper an apology. Explaining that he and his friends saw one another rarely and they were so enjoying being together once again. I would smile and ask him not to worry, that I loved merely sitting there, with no expectations, not even needing to think. Meaning what I said with every fiber of my being.

Earlier that afternoon, one of the men, a neurologist had shown up in the lobby of the hotel where I was staying. As I climbed into his small car, he said, "Andy thought you might like a tour of Crete." Then smiling, added, "And he told me you were a lovely American woman. One who knows medicine."

Flattery will get you anywhere with me. I returned his smile with a bigger one.

He drove slowly through the main roads of the small island. Slowly enough that I could take in this place which looked like it must have a hundred or a thousand years ago. Rolling hills dotted with small dark clapboard houses with porches. On each porch sat people who looked ancient. The small car made hardly any noise as we rode through the back roads of Crete. Off in my own world, I started when he drove into a parking lot. Explaining as we walked into the apartment building that he made the equivalent of sixty-thousand dollars a year and that he would like me to see his home.

"This is where my wife and I live." Extending his arms into an eight-hundred square foot room with dividers for cooking and sleeping. He smiled as he watched the evident wonder on my face.

"Most American college students have apartments larger than this, yes?"

I felt so many weird emotions. Embarrassment at the acquisitiveness of Americans like me and our consumer culture, coupled with profound gratitude for the man and his generosity, for Andy, for the beauty of this country and the joy of being here, the list was miles long.

As if reading my mind, he quietly said, "Coronary heart disease is rare here. We have no need for cardiologists or cardiac surgeons." Knowing, of course, that heart disease had been the number one killer of Americans for decades.

Following that first weekend in Crete, Andy dropped me off at the beach town of Talos where I was to stay for ten days. And then we would meet back up in Athens for the flight bank to the states.

I spent a week learning to enjoy solitary meals, including wine. And running a route I discovered above the beach while listening to Greek music. Then smiling at the flirtatious Greek men and writing a lot of poetry, I realized I could not leave this land without going to see the Acropolis, the Parthenon and the rock that Zeus split. That meant returning to Athens earlier than planned. And then figuring out how to get to Delphi. Tricky, because I spoke no Greek and most of the people I met here did not speak English. Even in the restaurants. And I had not told Andy that I would do this. No one would know where I was. A large part of the desire to take this trip alone had been curiosity about what it would feel like in a country where I knew no one. In fact, the desire was really a deep yearning for anonymity. So being in a place where no one knew I was had enormous appeal.

I took the bus back to Athens having decided to spend one night there before heading up to Delphi for the last three days of my trip. Once in Athens, I realized that dragging a suitcase around while searching for a hotel would be foolish so I hired a taxi. The driver spoke enough English for us to communicate, sort of. Finding a hotel for the night and buying the bus tickets for the ride to Delphi seemed the reasonable order of things. The taxi driver was most accommodating. Most likely because he did not think I would notice that we went down the same street at least three times. But he did do what I asked. Waited outside while I secured a room for the night then drove me to a different bus station from the one I had arrived from Athens to buy the tickets to Delphi. It would have taken hours for me to figure that out.

Once inside the bus station, determining which was the right one was somewhat dicey because I could find no ticket agents who admitted to speaking English. Three women merely looked blankly at me when I asked for some help. But from out of nowhere, behind one of the unhappiest looking of the three, emerged a smiling young woman who asked in excellent English if she could help me. She even directed me to the correct line for my bus to Delphi.

For the entire four-hour trip, I felt my excitement build. Delphi. The navel of the Greek world, home of the Oracle. I felt that I was traveling toward something rather than running away. I had finally admitted to myself that this trip had been running away from Randy, Hermann, Houston and the hundreds of knowing faces. Or so it felt. But this was something I was moving toward, I could feel it.

I am not at all sure what I expected to find in Delphi but without a doubt, the three days there were the highlight of my trip. It was early afternoon when the bus dropped me off. Given that Greece is a beautiful country, filled with majestic ruins and shadows of gods and goddesses, then Delphi is glorious, majestic, all of those indescribable adjectives and more. I wrote in my journal that the mountains were symmetrical. Rather than peaking, they literally roll into one another giving the impression of a single structure at its base with one continuous mountain top which undulates along the horizon.

The contrast with Athens was total. I had enjoyed the night in the capital and was pleased to have made the late afternoon climbs up to both the Acropolis and the Parthenon. But Athens had the universal feel of the city, frenzied, noisy and crowded. Regardless of the language, there is a unanimity to the city and its harried citizens. Delphi felt wholly different.

After dinner at a very nice restaurant near the hotel where I was staying, I lingered over a glass of wine watching the sun set behind the mountains. The densely vegetated land rolling down to the sea seemed to glow in the dying light. The air teemed with mystery and wisdom.

The center of Delphi is small with just a few shops, restaurants and a few places to stay in what look like bed and breakfast places. Randy had slipped a postcard into my suitcases before I left Houston. There were just two words on the card. "Gnothi Seauton." 'Know thyself' was inscribed on one of the walls of the forecourts of the Temple of Apollo according to ancient Greek writers. The maxim seems to be self-explanatory but after only a moment or two of reflection one realizes there are several possible meanings of the two simple words. Most famously, Socrates claimed in Phaedrus that he could not consider mythology or 'other irrelevant things' since he 'was not able as the Delphic inscription has it, to know myself'.

Several months before, I had read a biography of Socrates and found this quote surprisingly comforting. Sometime after I'd read the book, I had remarked to Randy that if Socrates did not feel that he knew himself, then I wasn't in such bad company. Apparently, he remembered.

Since it was early afternoon when we arrived in Delphi, I walked the half a mile route down the center of the village to the site of the Temple of Apollo. There were only a few people at the ruins when I arrived. The people in Delphi spoke English or were willing to give directions. Along the way, I noticed spectacular yellow sunflowers. The plants were very tall and the flowers large and brightly yellow. After seeing the sixth or seventh, I asked a man who was walking back from the ruins about them. Yes, he replied, they are called Athanatos. They grow only in sacred places and live an average of one- hundred- fifty years. They flower only once, he said, and then they die. Nodding in understanding at my astonished expression, he smiled and walked away. Six months later, I looked for the flowers in the beautiful meditation gardens in Kyoto, Japan. Another sacred place and beautiful but I found no yellow sunflowers.

I continued walking along the sidewalk heading to the ruins. Suddenly, there it was, looming along the entire mountainside to my left stretching up as far as I could see. The most striking feature the columns of the Temple of Apollo. Even in ruins, they were breathtaking, the six pillars reached toward the heavens, stirring the imagination with awe and wonder at what this once was. And I began to climb.

Upon entering the ruins, I stood among the columns wondering about the Oracle at Delphi or the Pythia as she was also called. Wondering about such potent women during an age and culture when the options of women were strictly limited. Curious, I thought then and still do.

We know little about the women who became the Oracles, just that they were considered to infallibly convey Apollo's wisdom to rulers seeking the outcomes of battles and kingdoms. Allegedly, the Oracle was of middle-age, a virgin and had been trained since childhood in the ways of the priestess. Her selection as a successor was based on some mystical rite of the order. Once asked to name the wisest man alive, the Oracle replied Socrates. To which he supposedly responded that her comment was based on the fact that he alone of all men was aware of the vastness of his ignorance. That interaction, say some scholars, provided the catalyst for Socrates' search for wisdom.

A few moments later in my climb, I saw the first of several egg-shaped rocks. Somewhat tall, the first sits in a protective enclosure on the boundary of the restored Athenian Treasury. The rock represents the site where the Oracle sat. An arresting sight.

One once again worth some thought. Along with the location of Delphi itself. When Zeus wondered where the center of the earth was, he set free two eagles one flying east, the other west. When they met in Delphi, then the God Zeus knew that here was the navel of the earth, Delphi.

The journey to Greece changed me. Not in ways I could readily describe when I returned or even now, looking back. I certainly looked the same, physically, but I felt altered in significant ways. There's a saying I use when writing about my fictional characters, comfortable in her skin. That's the closest I could get to the alteration. I learned in that far away land that home was not a person or a place. I felt a new confidence and excitement and curiosity about where my life was leading.

Kneeling alone in the woods on the sharp twigs and rocks in front of the rock that Zeus split, I prayed for the first time in many years. And relished the act of being on my knees in adoration. Without words because I did not know what words to use, nor did I know who or what I was praying to. There was merely yearning. And a decision to seek, or rather find God, figure out a way to have a relationship with him, or her, or it.

My last night in this breathtaking land of crumbled ruins, mystery, and ancient wisdom was listening to a concert in the stadium high above the ruins. For over two hours I sat on a twenty-five-hundred-year-old stone pew and listened to a Greek orchestra playing the Magnificat first by Bach and then Vivaldi. The music ended close to one in the morning, and I sat there alone while I considered these past ten days. The miracles of them, the privilege of being here. Then I walked back to my hotel from the stadium carefully picking my way down the sheer descent. The moonlight was brilliant and the silence so immense that I was confident I could hear the whispered prayers of the many hundreds of thousands who had worshiped in this place.

This sacred place.

CHAPTER NINE

A First

DURING THE LATEST RECONFIGURATION of senior administration at the hospital, much of what Harry had put in place was undone. At least for me, that was so. A former colleague had been brought in as a Chief Operating Officer. One of the many management levels that Harry had eliminated. Our management styles could not have been more different although we both had doctoral degrees from the same school, had the same first names just spelled differently, were both blonde and from a distance, could be mistaken for one another.

Therefore, Lynn's decision to fire me should not have come as a blow. But it did. The day after I returned from Greece, she told me I needed to leave and talked for over about thirty minutes about the numerous reasons why that was so declaring several times that I would be happier in a university setting and that she had secured a position for me with the Dean of the School of Nursing. When she finally wound down, she looked at me and asked why I was not saying anything. I was numb. Jetlagged, sleep deprived and emotionally drained from the recent conversations with Randy about who he was dating, I only wanted to get out of her office to get my head together. Lynn asked what I planned to do as I left her office. I did not answer.

I knew if the people at the new job got wind of this, I was toast. There would be no chance of my landing on their short list of candidates. I called a friend in the recruiting business for advice. Although there are thousands of hospitals in the country, academic medical centers were run by a relatively small group of people, some of whom enjoyed being the first to pass on a juicy piece of news. Acutely aware of this fact, Ruth suggested I go talk to a lawyer right away, just in case, she said.

I had not considered a lawyer. In fact, the idea had not entered my mind. But as I listened, I realized the value of Ruth's advice. She was speaking knowledgeably, using all the correct terminology like wrongful discharge and severance agreements. When I answered her questions about prior performance reviews, she laughed at how easily she felt I could qualify for a sizeable settlement from the hospital if I filed. I don't agree with the litigious nature of our culture and had no desire to file a lawsuit against the institution where I'd worked for seventeen years. When she asked if I would promise her that I'd go see a lawyer, I said I would. Then she asked if I knew someone I could trust but who was outside the politics of the hospital and medical school. Indeed, I did. I got on the phone and secured two appointments for the following day.

I paid two-hundred dollars to be told by a total stranger that it would be her pleasure to represent me if I chose to go forward with the suit against the hospital. She knew several people at Hermann, including Randy and listened to me explain the events of the past several months interrupting only a few times to clarify dates or times. The attorney added that she had practiced law for eleven years and not met a client who could successfully negotiate their own severance agreement until that morning. We shook hands, smiled at one another, and I left, feeling almost good.

"Call David and tell him you want to meet with him tomorrow."

I was now sitting in Steve Linder's office. He was telling me to call the CEO at the hospital where I worked.

Steve also had listened carefully and had said next to nothing until I had finished my story.

Surprised, I said, "On a Saturday morning Steve?"

"Right."

"I don't think he'll meet with me, Steve."

My former advisor and now I knew, friend's, face was hard. His expression one of resolve. It's a peculiar feeling when your back is against the wall with scarcely no options. And then realize just how alone you are. I had not been here before. Aware of how really terrible this would be if I had children or others depending on me. But then when someone unexpected steps in not only with care and concern but with practical, useful counsel, the depth of gratitude feels bottomless. I was astonished at the depth of the concern apparent on Steve Linder's face. "Call him, he will meet with you." And I did exactly that.

That night, Randy came over to the house. He said he was there to pick up some of his things he had left behind. But after he angrily left, I suspected he had been anxiously seeking information. Perhaps Lynn even asked to check with me to see what was on my mind. I realized now, even in my jumbled state of mind, that I was not powerless.

Initially, our conversation was civil, albeit awkward. But when I replied that I was not going to consult with him about anything related to Hermann, Randy began to get annoyed. Honestly puzzled, I told him that we were on opposite sides of this thing. No way was I going to think out loud with him or reply to any of his probing questions. But of course, it was the truth. His job was to protect the institution, mine was to protect me. That Lynn's decision to fire me came after Randy and I were no longer together was not lost on me. And there would have been extensive discussion about the conversation, at least among David, the CEO, Lynn and Randy, the hospital lawyer. I could imagine Randy predicting to both administrators that I would most likely accept the decision and quietly clean out my office.

Therefore, when I told him that I had gone to see a lawyer that morning, he completely lost his temper and began to shout asking how I could conceive of doing such a thing and was I planning to sue the hospital? It should have been a comedic scene, but no one was laughing.

Again I did not sleep very much that night. When David had readily agreed to meet with me at the time and place that I suggested, I knew I needed to carefully prepare what I needed to say, how to say it and clearly convey what I wanted. That night I got on my knees once again. This time, on my living room floor, the prayer directed at an oil painting I had bought in Santa Fe two years before, long before Randy and I had split up. Right, an oil painting. Here is the story about *Sunset at Red Gorge* by artist Poteet Victory that I was on my knees in front of that night.

Following Harry's sudden departure on the morning of my dissertation defense, there was considerable controversy surrounding the question of what to do for a CEO. Although the four of us Vice-Presidents felt more than adequate in handling things until a new CEO could be found, the Hermann Board was uncomfortable with such an arrangement. For several months, the Chairman of the Board functioned as CEO. Walter, the son of generations of oil magnates in Houston, decided to pull the senior members of the battered administration together for a several day motivation, team building, and general recovery session during the early weeks of his brief post as CEO. During one of the free evenings, Randy and I were wandering around the lovely downtown area of Santa Fe and browsing through the many quality art galleries. I passed by one titled Sunset at Red Gorge and stood there as if nailed to the floor. Words cannot convey the intensity of my conviction that I was looking at the face of God in this painting so I will not attempt to do so now. Suffice to explain that it took many minutes for me to stop sobbing because of the confluence of emotion that overwhelmed and paralyzed me. I spent more money on that oil painting than I had ever had before or since. It hangs in my bedroom now, a reminder of the astonishing ruses that God uses to get our attention.

That Friday evening, kneeling in front of the painting, I was unambiguous about whom I was praying to and what I was praying for. I begged God for strength, clarity, and courage the next morning. And the proper word was begging. Strength because I would be doing something at this meeting that I had never done before. Clarity because I knew I my tendency for verbosity and courage because I appreciated how critical was this meeting. For me, not David or Lynn. I understood why she had said the things she did. And in many ways, she was right. I was not happy at work, hardly anything about my job brought me pleasure. And had not since the departure of Harry, the man who was fired on the day of my defense of my dissertation. These things are never easy for any of us, a lot of energy is accumulated and expended to face a person considered a friend and tell her she needs to leave after seventeen years. However, the claims she made to justify her decision were echoing in my mind. As they resounded, they gained form and substance.

"Lin, no one is questioning your competence." David had been listening to a list I had put together the night before. The list enumerated the highlights of my last few years in senior administration. The people, situations, and problems I had taken on and handled when few others could or would have done so. His tone and facial expression revealed annoyance, impatience, disdain at what he was hearing.

We were sitting at a coffee shop not too far from the Medical Center. David had made an attempt at a social pretense of why we were there. Smiling, he asked how I was doing and did I enjoy the trip to Greece. Perhaps way too abruptly, I had cut him off and curtly explained why we were here. And I had not smiled back. I was nervous, had an agenda and needed to stick to it before I lost my nerve.

"Really? Do you honestly believe that?" My smile was more like a grimace as I looked back at him. To his credit, he looked away from me and at the table where our barely touched two cups of coffee sat.

"What do you want, Lin?"

His voice was soft; the irritability was gone. I heard the resignation in his voice.

"Get her off my back, David. Tell her to stop talking about me or my career to people inside or outside of the institution. When UMass calls you to ask about me, make use of this list to tell them what I did here. And tell Lynn to do the same." I never took my eyes away from his and saw a fleeting expression. There for just a minute and then gone. I was abruptly aware that he had expected me to ask for money. And that I could have named a sizeable sum. Ruth had been right. After all, there would have been at least one meeting between him, Lynn and Randy during the week. Especially after I had told Randy that I'd met with a lawyer. They had most likely agreed on the amount. Once again, this all felt like comedy but the Greek version. Where tragedy and comedy coexist.

"I think I'll be offered the UMass job, David. But there will be many more interviews as they drill down through the candidates." As I spoke, I grasped just how powerfully I intuited that I would be moving to Massachusetts for that job. So long as there were no complications from the institution where I had spent so many years. "I figure I'll be out of your hair this fall, late October or November. Until then, tell Lynn to act as if this past week did not happen."

I had been tense and worried as I drove to meet with the CEO of Hermann that Saturday morning. Yet I felt the strength, courage and clarity I had begged for the night before. As if it had been infused. This had been a first for me- the felt need to defend myself, my reputation. Always before, I had merely ignored gossip or people I had been told were 'out to get me.' But the stakes were way too high for me to ignore this. Strangely, I felt tangibly respect perhaps mixed with bafflement when David and I parted that morning. He must have considered me a fool for not asking for a settlement.

But I could breathe again. I was confident that the summer would pass without further problems between Lynn and me. And there was a deep reservoir of trust in myself that had not been there before.

CHAPTER TEN

The Search in Earnest

I KNEW I NEEDED some structure for this growing desire for a relationship with God. I had tried many versions of unstructured through the years: My own version of Buddhism and meditation, many self-help spiritual writers and counselors, a program called The Way, based on Gurdjieff during a weekend retreat with friends in California, Unity Church and tried returning to the Episcopalian Church. None of them lasted. Because I did not feel that I belonged.

So when my friend Libby suggested I go with her and her family to the Unitarian Church, I jumped at the offer. Libby had been an employee and became a close friend, closer after we were no longer in a boss-employee relationship. But that last summer in Houston, she spent untold hours listening and caring.

Most of that entire summer, I attended that Unitarian Church usually with Libby but frequently alone. Often crying quietly in gratitude that I was finally taking steps to get a relationship with God. I had been surprised when I read a comment about how important that was becoming in my journal. It had been written over a year ago.

I began to read about the Unitarians, their beliefs and how

the religion was founded but was mostly content to be at the Sunday morning service with others who were trying to get close to God. They had a library for new parishioners, and I borrowed a couple of books to learn about the beliefs and history. The ritual was consoling. Sunday morning cup of coffee, dressing for the service and merely being in the presence of others.

Things at work were heating up. Despite the rumors that I was the candidate for the UMass job, their offer had not been extended. In late July, I had returned for three days of interviewing with the medical department heads and a couple of Board members. The sense that I would be moving there was even stronger than before, but the actual call did not come. By September, the carefully orchestrated compromise between Lynn and me was fraying. Administrative meetings were an endurance test and Randy's office remained directly in my path as I walked to and from meetings. When we met in the hallway, the strain between us was evident.

Physically, I was in better shape than I'd ever been. I ran most every day and worked out with weights at a fitness club. Anxiety and grief can be remarkable aids to one's workout regime. Once Randy had told me he was dating then I began to do so as well. I winced when Randy said he was dating a lawyer he met at the wedding of a friend of mine, a few years earlier.

My friend Tim was a devout Jehovah's Witness and the wedding and their wedding vows wholly traditional, including Tim's new wife's promise to love, honor and obey him. That was the wedding where I behaved like an unmitigated ass. When I heard the word obey it incited an antireligious rant from me, not a mumbled comment but a tirade loud enough to be heard by many of the wedding guests. Had I an excuse such as too many drinks causing too little thought, my reckless words could have been somewhat overlooked but the wedding was in the early afternoon, and I had consumed no alcohol. The psychiatrist Jamie had been correct when she observed that I had what she called serious unresolved 'issues' with men and marriage.

Finally, the call came. Would I fly out in the next week so that I could begin looking for a house? And then the going away parties started. My favorite was assembled by the people who had reported directly to me. There they presented me with the Doberman puppy I had told my administrative assistant I hoped to buy. And a certificate they claimed had never before been awarded, I was a naturalized Texan.

The puppy and I flew into Logan airport late on a Saturday afternoon in early November. I fell wholly in love with that dog when I went to get him out of the airplane kennel he had been in for over eight hours. I had named him Ally, a shortened version of the breeder's line but had spent only a few weekends with him. I had only a vague idea of how to get to Worcester from Boston and was exceedingly nervous about all that was crashing down on me simultaneously. But that little dog, then he was about thirty pounds, maybe less, stood there on his ridiculously big feet, outside his kennel, wagging his tail and looking up at me with a look that seemed to combine excitement, adventure, and love.

So we flagged down a bus and asked how we got to the car rental agency. People were wonderfully friendly and smiling as they pointed the way. In the bus, I held him as we drove to the other side of the airport. He never barked or wiggled or tried to get down. Ally merely sat comfortably in my arms and then jumped into the rental car and sat on the passenger seat, and looked over at me as if to say," Okay, let's do it."

Man, I thought, this little guy has got to be scared to death. He's left his momma and all his siblings for the first time and seems mellow as can be. If he can act like this, so can I.

Fifteen minutes later when I figured out that I had taken a wrong turn and was heading the wrong way for the Mass Pike, I slowed my car down to a dangerous crawl. Then leaned out my window as I blew the horn to get the attention of a man passing me. The man blinked a few times, startled, then laughed as he listened to me explain that we had just flown in from Houston, Texas and asked if he could tell me how to find the Pike. The dog had moved over closer to me so he could see both of our heads. In a thick Boston accent, the kind man said, "Follow me, I'm going to turn around, and when I put on my right blinker, that's where you'll get on the Pike."

And our new adventure began. Before leaving Texas, I had found a trainer living in a nearby town who would keep and train the puppy during the week, knowing that my working schedule would be hectic. Ally was housebroken but still very young. I would pick him up on the weekends for the first few months.

I was at work the following Monday, two days after leaving Houston, disoriented but there. Countless times that first couple of weeks, I would be walking down a main corridor of the hospital, and from a distance, call out a name, thinking the man was a friend from the medical school at Houston. When he turned around, I would smilingly recover, introduce myself and sometimes, gain a new friend. Embarrassing, to say the least, but in a few weeks, this disappeared. The honeymoon period lasted almost a year. People were wonderfully cooperative and welcoming. There were problems to be sure, but it was clear that everyone in senior management wanted this to work. After all, extensive time and money had been expended in the decision process. And there was an upcoming very important site visit from the powerful Joint Commission of American Hospitals. Everyone was anxious about the five-day visit expected in several months.

The house I had rented in the adjacent small town of Paxton was perfect. Only eleven miles from the hospital, my commute was barely twenty-five minutes. There was a good sized forest in the back of the house for my rapidly growing Ally boy where we wandered through the snow on weekends. Perfect for when he lived with me full- time and I could rely on him coming when I called. My neighbor was also the realtor who had shown me the rental house when I flew up to find somewhere to live. Although it was the first home she showed me, I knew that was the place as soon as I walked in the house. When I stood in the living room looking out through the glass sliding doors through to the forest. I could 'see' the dog and me there in that room watching the snow fall and listening to music.

The house was small, bigger than the one I'd had in Texas but not by a whole lot and it felt cozy. I loved it at first sight. At the suggestion of a woman who had hosted a workshop for females about intentions that last summer in Houston, I had written three 'intentions' on small pieces of paper and then had crunched the strips of paper so they could fit in the windows of the house in Paxton. There were three. A close relationship with God, love and peace. The day John helped me move out of the house and into his, he found several of the scraps of paper not telling me for many months after we were married.

It turned out that Sue, the realtor, was my next door neighbor. She and her husband Warren could not have been friendlier. Even better, they had a little girl who loved dogs and was more than willing to take Ally for walks when I was tied up with a long day. In fact, they insisted on keeping the puppy for me that first night because it was so late when we finally made it to Paxton. They had been watching for me to get there and both were at the house right away even though it was after ten at night. After I had offered a tepid objection which Sue and Warren emphatically overrode, I let them take the boy and his crate and fell into bed.

Within a few weeks, I had found a Unitarian Church in the center of Worcester and attended each Sunday. The First Unitarian Church in Worcester, Massachusetts is over two hundred years old built in a classically New England architectural design with its tall white steeple and brick and white columned façade. The inside starkly severe with one exception. A friend from Houston had given me the name of her brother who played the organ for the church. And what an organ. The massive pipes of the organ dominated an entire wall of the cavernous church with a sound that seemed to resonate through my soul. The dog and I had our Sunday schedule set. By seven, we were out running the hilly streets, giving me plenty of time to shower, dress and get to church. There every Sunday, almost without exception, I sat and cried through most of the service. Weirdly happy to be back in church, any church and on my knees in any pew.

It was the Director of Nursing at UMass who suggested that I might be interested in a physician and practitioner of Ayurvedic Medicine named Abbas Qutab. I had asked Anne, which gynecologist she went to and she had told me about this man. Surprised but intrigued by what she had to say about him, I decided to go see him as there were some minor problems I had been ignoring since I'd left Texas. He was unlike any other doctor I had ever known. His office wall was plastered with credentials from just about every discipline one could think of, ranging from Chiropractic through Internal Medicine, Naturopathy, and Ayurvedic. When we first met, Abbas explained that he had completed his residency in Internal Medicine in London only to realize that it "wasn't enough."

His primary diagnosis of me was anxiety. All he ever did was palpate my pulse in both my wrists and talk with me to ask about my general health and habits. Listening to everything I said, he advised that I run less and take some yoga to relax me. There was no extensive physical exam or blood work. My hormonal problems were incidental and could be easily fixed, but he had a great deal to say about the anxiety. I was stunned. Anxious? Me? But he got my attention.

A month or two after we'd had that conversation, I was on my way to meet a blind date and decided to stop in to ask him if he had some time. It was late on a Friday afternoon, and he came out when he heard me asking the receptionist if he were in. When we got to his office, I extended my hand to ask if I was less anxious. Laughing, he asked where I was going. At my apparent puzzlement, he gestured at the dress I wore. Flustered, I explained that I was going on a blind date.

Nodding, Abbas then asked, "What are you looking for in a man?"

Floored because I had never had any experience like this-anything like this with anyone, I just stared at him. Dr. Qutab merely stood quietly regarding me while he waited for my reply. As I stood there, I was astonished when I realized I had never thought about this question. What was I looking for in a man? Why? Because I rarely admitted to myself that I was indeed looking for a man, a mate.

Finally collecting myself enough to answer him, I did. And talked for a few minutes.

Dr. Qutab shook his head as if to dismiss my carefully thought out answer to his question. And just said, "That's too philosophical an answer. Think about what kind of man you are seeking. The question requires only a few word answer."

For the first time in my life, I realized that men had always sought me out. At least the primary relationships. They had come after me. I had never given any thought to the kind of man I wanted to be with.

He smiled then and said, "Take your time."

I did. And thought about his question, the men I had been with and what they had been like. I blinked and said, "*Real.* I want someone *real.*"

Qutab nodded, this time with approval.

I had negotiated the two-week trip to Japan as part of my taking the new job. My friend Libby and her Japanese husband Ken had invited me to join them for a Christmas trip to Japan. A remarkable trip for we stayed first with Ken's parents in the suburbs of Osaka, then visited his brother and wife in Kobe. Libby's sister-in-law was Shinto, and we were invited along with her when she visited her father's grave on New Year's Day. She placed several of his favorite items near the small rectangular stone marking his grave. Later when we returned to her home, she offered us a view of the Buddhist shrine she had created for her dad in a corner of her bedroom. Simple and beautiful, it consisted of a statue of the Buddha, a photograph of her father, prayers beads and a candle which she lit while she honored him. When I moved into my rental house in Massachusetts, I created a similar one for my parents.

On the way back from several days skiing in the Japanese Alps, we stopped at Nara and spent almost the entire day wandering through the beautiful temple with what is said to be the largest statue of the Buddha in the world. A few weeks before the trip, a dear friend and former employee had died following a ten year battle with AIDS. Since the roof of the massive temple required frequent maintenance, some enterprising person thought up a clever way to finance it. Tourists could purchase replacement roof shingles and could write their own personal message on the shale. I bought one and wrote Blaise's name, along with a few words about how much he was loved and the date of his death at only thirty-five. Unable to attend his funeral back in Houston, I imagined this small act would have caused him to smile and provided a small measure of consolation for me.

Then we took the train to Kyoto where we walked to one of the splendid Zen gardens. A few times in my life, Zen Buddhism had been of sufficient interest to me that I had read books by Americans like Alan Watts in attempts to figure out the fundamental tenets of the philosophy. Much of what I read seemed over my head but as I gazed at the sand and stone garden in the temple, some of the tenets of Buddhism came back particularly detachment. Despite the presence of many other travelers, the stillness, and simplicity of the place elicited calmness and quiet even in Libby's six-year-old-child. The sense of reverence was tangible.

CHAPTER ELEVEN

Home—Finally

THE JOURNEY HOME BEGAN with a telephone conversation with a stranger. Early in that conversation, he asked what I was looking for, and I answered, " a sacred place," explaining that I had been to Kyoto, to Delphi, searching for something, I wasn't sure what. And the man who became my husband told me about St. Benedict's Abbey, in Harvard Massachusetts.

On lonely Sunday afternoons, I resumed my Houston practice of perusing personal ads with a bit of a twist. Much more careful now, I not only read what the man said he was looking for but listened to his voice on the taped message played when a caller dialed the identifying number. John Wilder had placed an ad which expressed interest in meeting a woman who was 'peaceable.' That word intrigued me as did his voice and name. Sometime in early February, I called the number provided by the newspaper hosting the personal ad service and was disappointed when I never heard a reply.

Easter Sunday morning that April of 1996 had been a typical Sunday in that the dog and I had gone for a run together and then I had gone to church where Will and his amazing choir sang The Canticle of the Sun. I had heard of neither the music or of Saint Francis, upon whose poem it was based. It was one of the most beautiful choral pieces I had ever heard. As was my custom, I cried through most of the service. Since it was Easter Sunday, I decided to go out for breakfast and lingered over the paper and my coffee, thinking that my life was settling into a comfortable routine. Being back in New England was finally easier. Not the feeling of being back with 'my people' that a friend from Texas had predicted, but I was building a life, alone with my dog. And felt content with the church I attended and the friends I was making.

The puppy was growing quickly, and I now was able to take him with me in the new Explorer I had purchased for the punishingly severe winters of western Massachusetts. A winter, I was told, which had brought the heaviest snowfall in several decades. He sat happily in the passenger seat of the SUV and was great company.

Although the snow was initially novel after so long in Houston, the constancy of the storms along with the very short periods of daylight got to me. Each morning when I awoke, it was dark and dark again at the end of my day. The idea of spring and all that it promises was intoxicating. After church, I drove the short distance home planning to grab my Dobie boy and take him for a run off leash in the woods behind my house when I saw the blinking light on my answering machine indicating that I had a message. Since it was not uncommon to be called at home about a problem at the hospital, I decided to listen to it before leaving again.

It was John Wilder calling to apologize and ask if we could talk. It seemed he had placed the ad a few months ago and then was so busy that he neglected to check his box for replies. In fact, he had just listened to the collection of messages from women responding to his ad. There were quite a few, he explained ruefully since it had been over three months since he had called the message service. Yes, he would like to talk to me, in fact, he would *love* to talk with me. Yes, I sounded interesting, more than interesting. Could I possibly call today? He would be home all day because he was cooking a braised beef and it took forever.

Without removing my spring raincoat, I called him, intrigued by the voice with a thick Boston accent, the energy, excitement and vitality which seemed to pour through the phone line. John answered the phone on the first or second ring. And was exactly the way he had sounded in the message. We talked for over seven hours that day.

Although I invited him over to my house after several hours on the phone, he asked that we wait to do that. Explaining that if we were not careful, we could miss that most significant, even central phase of a relationship between a man and a woman. The one where we take the time to learn about the desires, ambitions and most private fears of a person. Learn to trust or in a word become friends. That if this phase was rushed that it could not be retrieved. Although he never said the word sex, he did not need to because his meaning was clear. I was more than fascinated. This guy was like no one I had ever talked to before.

Within less than ten minutes, our conversation switched from the superficial like jobs when he said he was a Psychologist for combat veterans and that he attended daily Mass to deep-rooted subjects that I'd not talked about before. Despite my knee-jerk negative reaction to the notion of his being a 'shrink,' the end of his statement sparked a variety of reactions, uppermost among them, admiration, respect and a mumbled reply, "You do real work." Thinking of my twelve-hour days which were crammed with meetings, many of which felt pointless. Realizing that I disliked a lot of what I did because it did not feel like real work. So concentrated on my picturing the difference between our two jobs that I missed what he'd said next.

"What did you say after you told me what you do? Sorry, I missed it."

"That I go to Mass every day."

Still, I can picture me standing in my pink raincoat beside the bar dividing my small kitchen from the living room, floored by what John had just nonchalantly said. Too engrossed in the conversation, I had not yet stopped to remove my coat.

Mass every day. Huh? Daily Mass? It sounded strange, so weird that I had no idea how or what to say in reply. So I said nothing at all. John must have known how peculiar that was…or maybe not. It's a funny thing that when many of us do or do not believe or practice something, we assume we're in the majority. That everyone thinks like we do. Once while Randy and I were at one of the many black and white tie dinners back in Houston, I was sitting next to the Chief of Neurosurgery, Guy Clifton, at the medical school.

Although we worked together almost on a daily basis, we knew next to nothing about one another since we talked only about matters related to the hospital. Waiting for the program to start, we sat chatting, making idle conversation about current books and movies. When I asked Guy what his favorite book was, I expected to hear some well-known book on the New York Times Best Seller List. But quickly, without needing to think about it, he replied *The Problem of Pain*. Surprised that I had not heard of the book or the author, I had leaned closer to him to ask about it. Just as the program began, Guy whispered, "CS Lewis. It's about Christianity. I'm Catholic." The astonishment I had felt at a medical department chairman stating that he was Catholic was equaled by John's daily habit of church.

Why? Because somewhere along the way, I had decided that religious people in general, Christians in particular, were on the whole, irrational, even stupid. How else could anyone believe in the Bible, troglodytes like Pope John Paul ll, or be opposed to a woman's choice to having a baby?

I had never heard a man speak as John did. Say outrageous things which somehow did not sound shocking at all. They seemed, right.

As we talked, I thought of that conversation with Dr. Abbas Qutab just a week earlier. This man was clear...real. The exact word I had finally said when Qutab had asked what I was looking for in a man, real. Would John have found my three-month-old message if I had not been urged by Qutab to be explicit, definite? Intentions.

"What are you looking for?"

"A sacred place." I had not stopped to think, the reply just fell out of my mouth. And I turned to look at the materials I had sent for sitting on the table in the living room. Swimming with the dolphins would be an unforgettable spiritual experience, the ad had promised. For just under a few thousand, one could fly to Florida and spend seven days with these extraordinary animals. I had received the packet of information only a few days before but had been disappointed when I got them. In my reaction, not in what the promoters had to say. I had realized this would be merely another distraction, an expensive one at that. So when I heard those words leave my mouth, I realized yes, that was exactly what I was looking for.

John had waited for more after I answered him. Rather than asking for details, what do you mean? Sacred how? The sudden silence between us apparently did not bother him.

Smiling to myself as I thought, *shrink*, I explained into the silence, "I have been to Delphi and Kyoto but am still looking. I'm not really sure what I am looking for, but I think I'll know when I find it." Gave a self-deprecating laugh and described the swimming with dolphin trip I had considered. Rather than laughing along with me, John's reply was thoughtful, serious. It was apparent by his tone and comments that he considered this matter serious. And then he told me that he went to daily Mass at St. Benedict's Abbey in Harvard. It certainly qualified as a sacred space, people went there for weekend retreats, he knew and then he gave me the name and number of a monk who could answer my questions and schedule time to go there. The Abbey was, he estimated, about a forty-five-minute drive from my house. It's only thirty miles or so from you, but the fastest way to get there is to take the back roads.

I was excited on so many levels that I could barely contain myself. We had talked on the phone for over seven hours. I had a plan, not anything that I could coherently explain because this was all visceral, I was deliriously happy. Had a direction, would go see a monk named Father Xavier at the monastery as soon as I could possibly do it. And John? Definitely, a guy who marched to his own drummer.

I could not get the time off to get to the Abbey for a few weeks, after speaking with me for a few minutes, Father Xavier suggested I come out to spend a weekend. That way, the priest explained, I could get an authentic sense of the Abbey, perhaps more readily access what I was looking for. Father Xavier was matter-of-fact but friendly. Kind of like John. Thick New England accent, not really abrupt but sounded as if he did not have a lot of free time. As if he dealt with requests like mine every day. Maybe he did.

Between that Easter Sunday and two weekends later, I got to the Abbey, John called every night. At all kinds of times. We continued to talk about all sorts of things, and I liked him more and more. We still had not seen one another.

I drove up to the Abbey on a Friday afternoon, planning to

stay there for the weekend. Father Xavier was charming. Long black robes were tied about a thin waist with what looked like rope. The habit flapped about his legs as he strode out to greet me and show me around the Abbey. Energy, vitality and warmth poured from his smiling face as he welcomed me. About an hour later, the priest had walked me all around the beautiful grounds, including the library in the basement of the main house, dining room, and chapel and the room I was assigned until Sunday. Explaining their Benedictine prayer and Mass schedule, Father Xavier smiled and invited me to Vespers beginning in a few minutes and Compline at nine.

The priest had given me a brief history of the Abbey as we walked around the grounds. There had been difficulty with Rome back in the sixties and seventies, he explained. But the doctrinal matters had been resolved and, he assured me, the Abbey was in concert with the Magisterium and Vatican. I did not understand most of what he talked about, but inwardly, I smiled because the rebellious history of the place felt so comfortably familiar. A sign of a fit maybe.

Looking back on those days, I can recall only my sense that I was following a map. An interesting road which held an incredible variety of intriguing thoughts, feelings, and sensations. Although what I was doing felt planned, at that time, I was not considering becoming a Catholic or marriage to John. At least not in those fully formed thoughts.

When I walked into Compline later that night, I understood none of the Latin the monks chanted as they stood in their unpretentious dark wooden pews. And although everything about the ritual was foreign, the shock at the sense of belonging was so overwhelming that I could only cry in response.

John had told me where he sat during the daily Masses he attended at the Abbey. I had sat there during Compline and again the next day, Saturday, there I was in the pew he said was 'his' at the seven o'clock. And suddenly, there John was, sitting next to me. After the Mass, he asked if I had seen the chapel of Our Lady of Guadalupe. I had not. So I gladly accepted his offer to show it to me.

We walked outside of the sprawling white wooden buildings that constitute the Abbey and down a steep expanse of grass, walking for about ten minutes in the morning sun. And then crossed down to a river where there stood a statue of Christ, arms extended, all in white. Staring at the impossibly beautiful scene, I had not noticed the chapel on my right. Once inside it was tinier than it had looked from outside. Perhaps two hundred square feet or less, with a statue of the Mother of God in front of a very simple wooden kneeler.

Neither he nor I had spoken for at least fifteen, maybe twenty minutes. When we went outside of the chapel, John sat down on a bench which sat in front of the statue of Christ and to the left of her chapel. And asked if I knew about Our Lady of Guadalupe. Not trusting myself to speak, I just shook my head no, I did not. And John told me about Juan Diego, the Aztecs, the roses in winter and the huge church which now stands in the place she asked for a church.

Walking John back up the hill, he asked what I was going to do for the day. I'm going back down to that chapel, I told him. I want to talk to her. Then it occurred to me that John may have wanted to get together, for a date or something. So I asked. His answer? "No, call me when you want to see me. Something is going on between you and God. I don't want to interfere."

Upon returning down to the chapel, I stood outside for a long time. At least fifteen maybe twenty minutes, aware that I was terrified. Something huge was happening here, and I did not understand it, any of it. Finally, I mustered the courage to walk inside and did the only thing I knew to do. Lay down prostrate in front of that altar and begged. "I'm not sure if you talk to failed Episcopalians but here I am, and I have no idea what I'm doing. Please help me."

I stayed through the weekend. And had no desire to eat. Although Father Xavier had shown me the dining hall and had explained the times for the three daily meals, I was not interested. Strangely when I attempt to remember exactly how I spent that weekend, I cannot. I have no idea how I passed those almost seventy-two hours. But it was not long after that, perhaps a month that I called Father Xavier to tell him that I wanted to become a Catholic. His response was such a lengthy silence that I wondered if we had lost the connection.

"Father, did you hear what I just said?" I asked finally.

Almost sputtering, the priest exclaimed, "But I thought you were already a Catholic!" I laughed but understood why he had assumed this because that first day, during that first conversation with Father Xavier, I had talked about a lot of Catholics, John Cardinal Newman, Blaise Pascal, Kahil Gibran. All those years of listening to Sister Marie Bernard and John Bradshaw.

That next week, I wrote this poem to describe how I had felt that first evening because I could do so only in poetic form:

St. Benedict's Abbey

Suddenly I was there
On my knees with
Quiet tears coursing down
My cheeks in response
To feelings which were
So long suppressed and
Now foreign and exquisitely

Incisive as they pierced
Through the years of
Protective armor donned so
Long ago when I
Walked away from God
How did I arrive here?
And why was I deserving
Of such pure faith appearing
Without preamble or good works?
And why God, have you found
Me worthy enough to know you?
Once more forgiving this oh, so
Grateful recipient of unmerited grace.

CHAPTER TWELVE

Commitments

THE CATHOLIC FAITH IS loaded with rules, prohibitions, commandments. At least to the uninitiated, like me, this is true. With time, they fade way into the background, the rules are hardly the goal. But that realization came much later for me. Of course, a few were the same rules I had walked away from as a teenager; regulations about sex, marriage, and divorce. And some were new- a male, celibate priesthood, and precise rules about birth control. Oddly, it was just these rules which were one of the main attractions for me. Living in one of the most permissive cultures of this country and perhaps of any nation, the rules were a tangible relief. Order versus disorder, structure, tradition, all welcome. Finally, right and wrong, good and evil, no equivocating.

In fact, that lack of equivocation was the primary foundation of my attraction to John. When we disagreed on a matter of which John felt strongly, he was frank to the point of being brusque, even harsh. Here are a couple of examples of brief conversations during those first few months.

John had come to my house for dinner, and we were talking about the things people do as they are getting to know one another after dinner and some wine.

One of us brought up the subject of abortion. I defiantly and defensively declared that I had had an abortion expecting John to do what most people had done and back right off. But John calmly looked at me and said, "I believe that abortion is a mortal sin." I recall blinking at him, stunned, yet eerily relieved.

Truth: we recognize it, even when spoken in a new language like 'mortal sin.' I had known exactly what I had done all those years ago, had known I was committing murder. But then I had lied to myself and others when I supported Planned Parenthood, Emily's List and all the euphemisms surrounding the entire Pro-Choice matter. Even chuckling with two female physicians at a Planned Parenthood cocktail party about the number of abortions each of us had had. I was lowest at one while the late twenty-something-year-old anesthesiologist laughingly said she'd had four. As I stared at this man, all those stupid justifications fell away. "Of course, you're right," I said or something like that, there could be no argument here.

Not much later, perhaps a week or two, we were once again at my house on a warm Sunday afternoon lounging about the pool. Just as I was about to dive in the pool for a swim, John was walking back into the house and carrying a tray of empty plates from the lunch we'd eaten. Suddenly, he turned to say, "If you think about what you were taught by your mother as a little girl, you'll agree that sex before marriage is a sin." He was right on both counts, he knew it and so did I. It was then that we began to think about marriage and the required annulment for me.

In each of my many earlier spiritual explorations, there had been something which bothered me, kept me from a commitment, perhaps it was the absence of rules. Although I had liked and respected the Episcopalian priest Clark, who had been so kind to me, the history behind the formation of the Church of England under Henry VIII was too great an obstacle for me to seriously consider a return to that faith.

I had learned a good deal from my study of Buddhism, in fact, I still use many of the meditative techniques I studied. But it seemed more a philosophy to me than a religion.

A few years before Randy and I split up, a good friend had invited me to a weekend retreat with fellow followers of Gurdjieff. Grace and I had connected on several levels when we began to work together in Houston, and our conversations were fascinating to me. Aware that I was searching for something she had lent me some books from her library. When I read the dense prose about the difficulty most of us have in perceiving reality, in achieving what Ouspensky, a disciple of Gurdjieff, called full consciousness, I recognized the truth implicit in the conviction that most of us go through life asleep. The reading was arduous and required intense concentration which I liked. Hard work always indicated that this was the path I should take.

The weekend conference was called The Suffering Christ and the Laughing Buddha and was led by a philosopher whom I knew, Jacob Needleman, and a French artist named Paul Reynard. I found the content and people so captivating that I planned to become a member of the Houston Gurdjieff group when I got back home to Houston. But when Grace's friend excitedly exclaimed as we were about to leave for the airport, "Lin, we're so happy that you're planning to join *The Way*," the visceral negative reaction I felt at hearing those words *The Way* was so powerful that I could not ignore it. There was something wrong here, a red flag so bright I could not ignore it. A few years later upon learning that Christ's early disciples referred to Christianity as The Way, I recalled that moment with more than a little wonder.

Finally, during the years of attending the Unitarian Church, there were a couple of obstacles for me there as well. I had read that the originators of the faith had done so in reaction to the notion of the Trinity. Similar to the Muslim religion, the early Unitarians considered the Trinity as offensive to the one God. But the church in Worcester expressed itself as "Trinitarian." This was puzzling to me, smacked of disorder or at the very least a lack of unifying principles. Furthermore, one of the primary axioms of that faith, that we use our human reason to find God served as a major impediment for me. For years, I had trusted my reason and been unable to find what I was looking for. Over the course of two years, I attended services at three Unitarian Churches but knew this was not my final stop.

The feeling I had about Catholicism was not something I could easily explain in words, to others or to myself then or now. And it made no sense because I knew nothing about this religion, it was never among the list of faiths I had tried on for size. I had never read any books or articles about the Catholic religion nor had I spoken with John in any detail about being Catholic. About why he was Catholic. Or even what he believed. I had accepted at face value his offer of the Abbey as the sacred place I was seeking. And once I got there, found not only a holy place but so much more. Crazily, I felt as if I had come home, after a long and exhausting journey. But- there's often a but when we achieve something momentous- I found myself second guessing myself.

Upon hearing my story, there were a few people assumed I was converting because of John. Certainly, that would be a natural enough guess. Because I too worried if that may be true. Maybe pleasing a new man was the unconscious, *real* motive in my decision to become Catholic. And perhaps this compelling sense of belonging was a new figment of my imagination.

I was sufficiently concerned that I took a risk with the head of the Visiting Nurses Association in Worcester. Gloria had been unusually friendly from our very first meeting. Nearing retirement, she knew the political lay of the UMass land and shared her knowledge liberally. Gloria was funny and shared her wisdom without being unkind to any of the major players and had clarified some confusing politics for me on more than one occasion. One day at a luncheon meeting with only the two of us, she mentioned that she was Catholic. I decided to take a chance and seek some advice from her.

I had learned very quickly that many people I encountered in Massachusetts called themselves Catholic but when I began to speak with them about my interest in the religion, would tell me that they no longer went to church. It was confusing. I had encountered similar contradictions only in my Jewish friends who were Jewish in name only. And I understood that was so because of the ethnicity of the Jewish people. If you are Jewish, usually, you are of Jewish heritage. But Catholic?

In this post-modern, post-Christian culture, many Catholics then and now felt the prohibitions are obsolete. And yet, these people identified so heavily with their Catholic roots that they identified themselves as Catholic. But not enough to go to church. After a few conversations with 'Catholics' and then being trapped into listening to a rant about their numerous reasons for not attending Mass, I no longer admitted to an interest in Catholicism.

This was also the mid-Nineties in Massachusetts. The scandals about predator priests from several decades earlier made daily headlines in the Boston Globe for the entire time I lived in Massachusetts. The almost universal animosity toward Bernard Cardinal Law was like nothing I had ever witnessed. The media concentrated a level of unadulterated hatred on this man that astonished me. Repeatedly, he attempted to explain that he had merely followed the then conventional thinking of psychiatry during the Eighties. Law's reasoning that he had arranged psychiatric treatment for the offending priest and then transferred him to a new parish because he had accepted the psychiatrist's declaration of cure was ridiculed and vilified. I never met Cardinal Law but was impressed by his strong support of Project Rachel, a program targeted at women who had aborted their babies. Project Rachel was one of the first of its kind in not only acknowledging the traumatic consequences of abortion to women but going much further.

The project consisted of a structured series of methods for women to open themselves to achieve forgiveness from the church and themselves. The latter was the real work I was to learn. But none of Law's accomplishments reached the public, only his 'protection of predator priests.' Catholicism in mid-Nineties Massachusetts was under fire.

When Gloria said she was a Catholic, I had asked if she practiced her faith. Curiously she had said, "Of course, why?" She nodded sadly in understanding when I explained some of my experiences with 'Catholics' at UMass. Something told me I could trust this woman so I leveled with her. Briefly, I covered the high points of why I left the faith of my childhood, the periodic attractions of other traditions and finally the weekend at the Abbey, the conviction to become Catholic. And then the fear that it was all to please a man, the religious fervor, another illusion.

She listened without asking any questions at all. And when I was done, she just said, "My husband is a spiritual director. Perhaps you would like to talk to him about this. He is semi-retired, works from home and I think would be happy to meet with you in your office."

Gloria's husband was kind, discreet and full of insight. Exactly as his wife had done, he listened carefully and interrupted me only to clarify the sequence of events. And then said the most intriguing thing to me. "The *journey* is classically male. If you consider Odysseus or any of the classic heroic figures, the tales are universally those of heroic male adventures, generally requiring sacrifice." Peering at me intently across the round table in my UMass office, he added, "But home is characteristically feminine. It is the woman who makes a home for herself and her family."

Indeed.

That night I looked in my journal for a poem I had written after that weekend workshop is California. After I had realized that Gurdjieff and his followers were not for me, I did not fit with them, I poured my disappointment into a poem. I called the poem Belonging:

Is there a place called home
Where memories and tradition await
Patiently hidden in places made deep
By relentless pursuit of useless truths.
Do we come trailing clouds of glory
Only to don the actors pose
And spend too many years and tears
Reclaiming wisdom lost so long ago
Saved finally by the knowledge
That human truth is shadow and illusion
Yet uplifted by one hope and prayer
That pure path toward peace and
Understanding lies patiently waiting
For our gaze to turn back to the
Place where we began?

Father Xavier could not take me on. Very apologetically he explained that he was Prior, which required numerous tasks as appointed by the Abbott. Among them was working with people like me, guests who wanted to use the Abbey as a place to escape or heal a wounded soul. But I inferred from his words that a guest who decides she wanted to become a Catholic was a rare phenomenon. Especially when it seemed by her initial conversation that she was already Catholic.

During that summer of 1996, I met with then Brother Andrew at least weekly. Father Xavier had said this pairing would work well for both of us because he was completing his thesis for a Masters in Theology at St. John's Seminary. Working with me would help him complete the last obstacle before his ordination, Father Xavier had said with a broad smile when he introduced the two of us.

Our first meeting was more than awkward. John thought the monks were a bit captivated by the fact that the Hospital Director at UMass was studying Catholicism at the Abbey. After all, many of them went to UMass for medical care. He suggested that Brother Andrew might be intimidated by his new task. So when Brother Andrew walked into the small room where I sat waiting nervously on an old tattered chair for our first meeting, I stood to greet him. He barely met my eyes. I extended my hand and waited until he took it. Then said something like, "Believe me, I am more nervous than you are. It's true I have a lot of education, but not much that's relevant to what we'll be doing here." Since the air still felt charged, I continued talking, trying to lighten the atmosphere.

" I did major in Philosophy, but that was a million years ago. I am just now reading the Bible for the first time in my life and understand scarcely any of it. But the truth is that I can barely spell Catholicism. I am hoping you can teach me how. Consider me a blank slate, please."

Brother Andrew looked nothing like any monk I had visualized. But then I had never known a monk, other than Father

Xavier, and he seemed to be in a class by itself. But I definitely did not picture a tall thirty-something man with dark wavy hair who was good looking enough to be an actor. That was Brother Andrew. My comments evoked a shy smile and a grateful expression on his face. I decided that was good enough to start.

And we got to it agreeing on a tentative schedule. We would meet for two hours each Saturday morning at a minimum. If I could free up the time during the week, we would meet an additional time like this first meeting on Thursday evenings.

One Thursday evening during a study session with Brother Andrew, he mentioned the Feast of the Most Holy Rosary as being October 7. Once again, I caught a glimpse of the immensity of the mystery and magnitude of God's love and plan. October 7 is my birthday.

It was not you who chose me, but I who chose you and appointed you to go and bear fruit that will remain, so that whatever you ask the Father in my name he may give you.

CHAPTER THIRTEEN

The Vocabulary of Faith

THAT SUMMER I READ four maybe five texts which were considered basic textbooks. Each was a tough read and required intense concentration. But unlike the Gurdjieff texts, this was familiar territory, more than that, it was fun. Fun. Really? Reading a textbook from the 1940s based on St. Thomas Aquinas' writings is fun?

My 'yes' is unqualified, unconditional. Can you imagine finding something you have been looking for most of your life? A something you could not describe even to yourself but once you found it, you knew? And even better, a teacher to guide you, answer your questions, one on the same path as you?

In his delightful book, *Mere Christianity*, C.S Lewis explains eloquently exactly the way I felt:

"Everyone has warned me not to tell you what I am going to tell you in this last book. They all say "the ordinary reader does not want Theology; give him plain practical religion." I have rejected their advice. I do not think the ordinary reader is such a fool. Theology means "the science of God," and I think any man who wants to think about God at all would like to have the clearest and most accurate ideas about Him which are available. You are not children:

why should you be treated like children? In a way I quite understand why some people are put off by Theology. I remember once when I had been giving a talk to the R.A.F., an old, hard-bitten officer got up and said, "I've no use for all that stuff. But, mind you, I'm a religious man too. I know there's a God. I've felt Him: out alone in the desert at night: the tremendous mystery. And that's just why I don't believe all your neat little dogmas and formulas about Him. To anyone who's met the real thing they all seem so petty and pedantic and unreal!"

Now in a sense I quite agreed with that man. I think he had probably had a real experience of God in the desert. And when he turned from that experience to the Christian creeds, I think he really was turning from something real to something less real. In the same way, if a man has once looked at the Atlantic from the beach, and then goes and looks at a map of the Atlantic, he also will be turning from something real to something less real: turning from real waves to a bit of coloured paper. But here comes the point. The map is admittedly only coloured paper, but there are two things you have to remember about it. In the first place, it is based on what hundreds and thousands of people have found out by sailing the real Atlantic. In that way it has behind it masses of experience just as real as the one you could have from the beach; only, while yours would be a single isolated glimpse, the map fits all those different experiences together. In the second place, if you want to go anywhere, the map is absolutely necessary. As long as you are content with walks on the beach, your own glimpses are far more fun than looking at a map. But the map is going to be more use than walks on the beach if you want to get to America.

Now, Theology is like the map. Merely learning and thinking about the Christian doctrines, if you stop there, is less real and less exciting than the sort of thing my friend got in the desert. Doctrines are not God: they are only a kind of map. But that map is based on the experience of hundreds of people who really were in touch with God—experiences compared with which any thrills or pious feelings you and I are likely to get on our own are very elementary and very confused. And secondly, if you want to get any further, you must use the map. You see, what happened to that man in the desert may have been real, and was certainly exciting, but nothing comes of it. It leads nowhere. There is nothing to do about it. In fact, that is just why a vague religion—all about feeling God in nature, and so on—is so attractive. It is all thrills and no work; like watching the waves from the beach. But you will not get to Newfoundland by studying the Atlantic that way, and you will not get eternal life by simply feeling the presence of God in flowers or music.

Each weekend, I was attending Mass with John, amazed at how like the Episcopalian was the Catholic liturgy and filled with joy each time I recited the creeds. Remembering all too well those times when I tried but could no longer narrate the prayers because I no longer believed. And now overwhelmed by the plain delight in proclaiming, "I believe in one God, the Father, the Son, and the Holy Spirit." How tremendously freeing it felt for me to stand there amidst a large number of men and women as they said The Apostle's Creed.

Although I could not yet receive Communion as a Catholic, I remembered clearly what those white wafers were, in reality. I knew the transubstantiation versus consubstantiation distinction about the hosts which became the Body of Christ and the wine which transformed into his blood. Strangely, it was one of the very few theological doctrines I dredged up from my Episcopalian confirmation class as a teenager. Whether the wafer and wine are symbolic only or actually did transform into Christ was a topic of controversy among Protestants and Catholics then and remains so today. Perhaps even more so now since even some Catholic priests are on record in their belief that the act is symbolic only.

But for me? There was no question. This was Christ, and I eagerly awaited the time when I could receive along with the other communicants. In my view, then and now, Catholicism is a package, either I am one, or I am not. Makes no sense to review a list of attitudes I agreed with versus those I did not. More on that in a later chapter.

Thinking back to those few months of study at the Abbey, I recall the pleasure with which I learned my introduction to this faith and the enjoyment of my discussions with Brother Andrew. My ignorance of all things religious was vast. Hence, the request to be treated as if I were a blank slate was hardly an overstatement. By necessity, what follows is an abbreviated list of the vocabulary, books, and principles that after almost twenty years still influence me.

Take sin for example. I had spent years living as a woman who did not believe such a thing existed. The ten commandments, like the Bible itself, was an anachronism. But once the defenses and rationalizations are put aside, the truth takes up residence and the relief of admitting the enormity of all the error is freeing. Paradox. Strangely, the longer I practice this faith, the more my ideas of sin deepen or maybe broaden. Initially, it's all about the rules, the ones I flouted, as I said in an earlier chapter. With time, prayer and study our conception of sin changes, sometimes radically.

And then there is the soul, my soul, yours and each human person. That I had one had not entered my mind in decades, if ever. I used the word, of course, in referring to people with whom I felt a deep connection as 'old souls' and for a time, thought of Randy, the lawyer in Houston, as my 'soul mate.' But the soul in this context was entirely different from those expressions. And the consequences of an entity like this staggered me. The bridge to eternal life, for the human person.

There was a time, and there were cultures, I suppose, when discussions about matters of faith were second nature for average people and used in daily conversation. When these issues were believed to be a grave matter to be taught, explored and accepted or rejected. From the view of the twenty-first century, they seem medieval, born of myth and superstition.

While in Europe several years ago, I thought of a different time as we wandered through the stunning, glorious, empty Cathedrals on every corner of Paris, Rome, and London. They seemed like museums, hundreds line up to await the opening of the tourist lines to view Il Duomo when they could see everything by just attending Mass. But a few centuries ago the prevailing culture was unambiguous: Everyone attended Mass. Was it easier to understand these weighty teleologic questions of faith when everyone went to church? When the cavernous Cathedrals were filled to overflowing?

How the soul integrates with the will, mind and spirit were complicated and confusing concepts to me, therefore, we spent two, maybe three sessions discussing an important principle of Catholicism. Brother Andrew was careful to emphasize the Catholic belief in the unity of body and soul. The quasi-equal relationship between the two. Aquinas sided with Aristotle in the anti-dualistic dispute that appears through the ages dressed up in facile phrases like Descartes' "I think. Therefore, I am." Suborning the body to an inferior place.

I had to think about that back then and do again as I write now. How very tempting it is to exalt the spirit and the intellect while dismissing our material selves or to at least relegate the body to the last place. But once I reflect for just a moment, Paul's admonition echoes in my head...the temple of the holy spirit. And I remember the most important point the Benedictine monk made about this complicated theology. We were fashioned by

God, all of us; what has been made by God is worthy of respect, even reverence.

Virtue and vice had not been in my lexicon. In my attempts to assimilate their meaning while I'd been studying Aquinas, I told Brother Andrew that virtue seemed very much like exercise to me. I meant that neither takes place without discipline, a discipline which over time, becomes a habit. The word vicious was, of course, familiar to me. But I had never considered its root word.

Reading the St. Thomas Aquinas book evoked the feelings I had experienced while in Delphi, Greece. There was no reason that the theories and ideas presented in the textbook should feel known, but they did

Following six weeks or maybe two months spent studying the Aquinas text, we completed the tome. Sighing as I handed back the worn book to the monk, I said, "I understood maybe ten percent of what is written in this book. Even after reading parts three or four times, I could not decipher the meaning."

Brother Andrew said, "You know St. Thomas never finished the Summa, don't you?" Without waiting for my answer, he said, "He stopped writing at question 99 on the third part of the Summa Theologica and never wrote again. When asked for an explanation, he said, 'All that I have written seems like so much straw compared to what I have seen and what has been revealed to me.'"

Yes. By its very nature, a word limits and bounds a thing. Never can it perfectly match the reality of it, no matter how well crafted the prose. Already, I found myself at a loss for words when I described how dear was this faith, how exquisitely precious. And how frustrated when I was unable to fit my fervor into a vessel of words so that another could taste and maybe even digest it.

Brother Andrew presented the next book for my study and our discussion with veneration. "This is Dom Marmion's classic, I think you will like this book."

Christ: The Life of the Soul remains in my personal library. Published in 1917, the book became widely read to the great surprise of its author, Dom Marmion. The book is best known for what Abbott Marmion called 'Divine Adoption.' At the beginning of the last century, the Catholic Church's conception of humans as divinely adopted by God the Father was not widely expressed as doctrine. The Latin Mass and the strict control by the local priests resulted in a laity which was mostly uninformed. For an Irish Benedictine Abbott born in the nineteenth century to take the writings of St. Paul and expand them into a book was a radical step. In fact, Marmion was shocked at the reception of the book by theologians and even Popes.

Over five times Paul uses that word adoption: In his Letter to the Romans, "the Spirit you received does not make you slaves, so that you live in fear again; rather, the Spirit you received brought about your adoption to sonship. And by him we cry, "*Abba* Father."

In Galatians, "But when the time had fully come, God sent His Son, born of a woman, born under the Law, to redeem those under the Law, that we might receive our adoption as sons. And because you are sons, God sent the Spirit of His Son into our hearts, crying out, "Abba, Father!"...and in Ephesians' "he predestined us for adoption to sonship through Jesus Christ, in accordance with his pleasure and will—" Stunningly effusive sweepingly broad statements which had not been assimilated into the dogma. It was this man who explicated the sanctifying grace by which "the substance of our souls are deified" as that which is recognized by God the Father as the essential first step in the supernatural adoption which permits us to call him Father. That sanctifying grace? Baptism.

Marmion carefully explains. For human adoption to take place, both adopter and adoptee must be members of the human race. But the adoption that the Apostle talks about is necessarily, "a marvel of the Divine Wisdom, power, and goodness. God gives us a mysterious share in his nature which we call "grace...an interior quality, produced in us by God, inherent to the soul, adorning it and making it pleasing to God, just as in the natural domain, beauty and strength are qualities of the body, genius, and science are qualities of the mind, loyalty and courage are qualities of the heart."

Once again, the Irish Abbott takes off from St. Paul's almost mystical passages about citizenship in heaven. 'So then you are no longer strangers and aliens, but you are fellow citizens with the saints and members of the household of God, built on the foundation of the apostles and prophets, Christ Jesus himself being the cornerstone, in whom the whole structure, being joined together, grows into a holy temple in the Lord. In him you also are being built together into a dwelling place for God by the Spirit." (Ephesians 2:19-22) Paul is talking here about the Mystical Body of Christ. A concept which did not become church dogma for another two thousand years.

This lion of an Apostle, perhaps the most fanatical of the Pharisees who persecuted Christians. And who went to the third heaven seems to have been gifted with understandings about Christ which were not understood until fairly recent times. Mind boggling.

When I read about the mystical body of Christ, I encountered yet another example of this strange déjà vu. I knew neither the phrase nor had the concept ever been introduced to me. And yet the 'of course' loomed in my mind. "Of course, this would be the way he designed all of this."

Although I had never conceived of the Mystical Body of Christ, a few pieces of the massive chessboard of the mystery of God clicked into place. All at once. We were all connected, all of us. Even if the virtual arteries and connective tissue had narrowed, even closed, due to sin, they were there. They existed. All of those strangers speaking to me through the years, even perhaps praying for me. There was no doubt in my mind, none at all. This was why I had felt this powerful sense of belonging, of being home. So much was made clear to me by this construct. But most of all the effects of our sins and of our goodness on the Body and on each one of us.

There were several more books on my reading and study list. A couple written by James Schall, a prolific Jesuit priest and an author I enjoy reading now along with Alistair MacIntyre's *After Virtue*. MacIntyre had written over half of his book when he discarded it and started over. A committed atheist and Marxist, the process of writing *After Virtue* revealed the errors of both Atheism and Marxism, the Scottish philosopher converted to Catholicism in the course of rewriting his book.

The vocabulary of faith is bottomless, the scope of works written about God by men and women, immense. But I had now a working language. Terms like theological virtues, cardinal virtues, gifts of the Holy Spirit, chastity and prudence were now familiar.

By late August of 1996, I told Brother Andrew that I was ready to join the church. I was ready. He seemed surprised that I wanted to stop our sessions, and I thought I understood why. However, we had never defined a program or time frame, from the beginning, this was a loose type of seminar. Quite candidly, I told the monk that I was fully aware that I had much to learn, that I would continue to take advantage of the endless treasures of wisdom. After all, there were centuries of tomes written about

Christ, the Church and the Saints. Impossible for a population to digest never mind an individual. But I wanted to get on with it. I knew I had things to do, and I needed to join the Church as a first step.

To his credit, Brother Andrew listened carefully to my reasoning and then agreed. We began to prepare me for the rites which would permit my entry into the faith. The sacrament of confession had loomed in the background for months, now it was here, and I was terrified, mortified, humiliated. How could I tell these men in black robes the really awful things I had done? Brother Andrew offered to do a 'roleplay' with me. Not yet a priest, he could not hear my confession nor give me absolution, but he was willing to offer sympathy, from one sinner to another. That was exactly how he portrayed it when I could not continue in the role play, I was crying too hard. The monk looked at me, not just with kindness but love and said very quietly: "Believe me, Lin, everything you ever did in your life before now, I have done too, or I have thought about doing. Underneath these black robes is a California surfer."

On September 5th, 1996, my mother's birthday, I received the sacraments of Conditional Baptism, Confirmation, Reconciliation and the following day received the Body and Blood of Christ. I was now a Roman Catholic Christian.

CHAPTER FOURTEEN

Why Catholic?

BACK IN THE DAYS when my mouth knew no editor, when the zeal of my new found faith was impossible to restrain, I had lunch with a hospital administrator in our hospital system who had called to check out the new Hospital Director from Texas. Initially, our conversation ranged through the safe, expected subjects of the executive life, budgets, layoffs, worrisome trends in academic medicine like federal cutbacks in funding. He seemed like a really nice guy and was curious about what I thought of Massachusetts after all those years in Texas.

His eyes widened while I explained that I had recently become a member of the Catholic Church, that it was the very best decision I had made in my entire life.

Hardly the reply the man expected in response to such a casual question. But my enthusiasm knew no bounds. Enthusiasm in the original meaning of the Greek word: Possessed or inspired by God. Finally, in a desperate attempt to change the subject, he said he'd been an altar boy as a kid and that he guessed he understood my attraction to the Catholic Church, "if you like living in the fifth century."

Indeed.

Judy, Chris and I had reconnected after many years and were having lunch at a restaurant accessible to Chris from Hartford, Judy from Brookline and me from Leominster. There was a lot for the three of us to talk about because I had not seen either of them for a couple of decades. Both women knew that I had been recruited from Houston for the UMass job, and each offered advice about the politics of the place. Once the professional side of things was exhausted, either Chris or Judy looked at me to ask what else was going on in my life.

The broad grin nearly split my face in two as I announced, "I've become a Roman Catholic."

Chris's face was a study in shock and Judy took a sip of wine and commented dryly, "That figures Lin, people are leaving the Catholic Church in droves, and you decide to become one."

For the remaining two years that I held the job of Hospital Director at UMass, any private conversation with me which lasted longer than a few minutes educed this kind of response.

Even during a breakfast meeting with the new CEO of the new merger between UMass and the major private hospital a mile down the street from the UMass campus. The merger occurred about a year after I had held the position of Hospital Director at the medical center. The merger had been predicted for a while, long before I had arrived, but anxieties were high throughout the entire organization. Dr. Levine was the brand new CEO of the newly created UMassMemorial Health Care System. I had met Peter Levine before at a few ceremonial, social occasions but had not ever spoken at length with the man. I should have been nervous. There could have been only one reason for the meeting. And that was to decide on my suitability for the job of CEO of both hospitals. There were two hospital directors, and the new system had need for only one. Word on the street was that my colleague at the Memorial would not be the new Director with the job title upgraded to CEO.

He could not have been more charming during the first few minutes of the meeting, liberally complimenting me on what I had done over my first years at UMass. And then came 'the question.'

"What would you say is the most important thing to you in your life right now?"

Without blinking or thinking very hard about what he asked, I replied, "My faith."

Covering his shock with aplomb, he asked a few questions, but they were most likely perfunctory. The meeting ended shortly afterward.

By this time, John and I were engaged to be married, in July of that year, and I told him about the conversation with Peter at dinner.

"You realize, I hope, that you have just shot yourself in the foot with that response, right?" Smiling, he grabbed my hand, "But I'm sure proud of you for answering his question that way. That was gutsy, maybe stupid regarding your career and its future at UMass, but courageous. I don't know if I could have answered that way."

But there was no other way I could have replied to that question. Because no other answer comes even close to the truth. I knew it had little to do with courage on my part, more an inability to stifle the almost constant bubbling over of the joy I felt. This faith, this precious gift that I so wished could be infused into each one of us, was irrepressible.

When Anne, the Director of Nursing at UMass, confided that she too was Catholic and gave me a lovely painting of the Mother of God with the Christ Child in her arms, I thought nothing of displaying it on my office wall. And when a member of the basic science faculty at the medical school dropped dead while on a business trip in Germany, I did not think twice when I began the weekly department head meeting with a request for prayer and silence for the soul of Dr. Fay.

However, a request from a close friend of Brother Andrew's did cause me tremendous anxiety. If I accepted his invitation and went, my presence would, I knew, be noticed in the very liberal and secular culture of UMass. Bill Heisner was a third-year med student and appeared in my office to inform me that he had attended the ceremony at the Abbey when I became a Catholic. He hoped I didn't mind, but Brother Andrew had invited him. I sat smiling at this earnest young man murmuring that of course I didn't mind and waiting for the other shoe to drop. This would be huge. I just knew it.

But nothing could have prepared me for what he was there for. Bill explained that he and a handful of other med students were Christians and had invited Dr. Bernard Nathanson to participate in a forum about abortion. They were very excited because the UMass faculty and administration was heavily Pro-Choice and the students believed that a debate with a man like Dr. Nathanson may provoke second thoughts among those who had not given the matter a lot of thought. They would show Silent Scream, the movie that Dr. Nathanson had produced to educate the public about the fetus. A movie which graphically and explicitly exposed the lies we tell ourselves about the procedure of abortion and its impact on an unborn child at three months old. Oh, he excitedly added in his lengthy narrative, did I know that Bernard Nathanson had recently converted to Catholicism? And ended with his request. He had informed the group of med students he was working with that I had become a Roman Catholic. He was there on behalf of the entire group. Could I attend this forum? It would make such a difference if the Hospital Director could come.

With no effort at all, I vividly remember my completely oxymoronic reaction as I listened quietly to this heartfelt request. While part of me was thinking, "Of course, something like this would happen, it was almost predictable, "stand up and be counted, put your money where your mouth is"...like that. While the other part, the predominant chunk was terrified, with a viscera suddenly filled with ice.

Bernard Nathanson, a self-proclaimed 'Jewish atheist,' was one of the leading figures in the political pressure resulting in Roe v Wade, legalizing abortion in the US and founder of NARAL Pro-Choice America. Either he or one of his residents had performed my abortion in 1973. I knew this because St. Luke's Hospital in New York City was one of the few hospitals where abortion on demand was available in the country. Once again, I was face-to-face with a self I found impossible to forgive.

Most likely because of my pallor and silence, Bill intuited my distress and hurriedly concluded his meeting with an apology. Something like I know how busy you must be, and I am sorry to have placed another burden on you or words to that effect. But, of course, I had to appear at this forum. It was the very least I could do to show support for these courageous students, for what they were trying to do. I took a week of vacation that week and hoped that if I turned up in jeans, and sat in the far back row of the auditorium, my presence might go undetected. Of course, in the opening minutes of the program, the Associate Dean of the system's gaze found me and stayed there long enough for me to notice him. Take note of his notice.

Did these things contribute to the mutual decision one year later that I did not fit the corporate image of the new system? Probably. It's not smart to flaunt the values of your employer. Certainly not my intention but that had been the impression at times like this one.

But sacrifices like these do not go unnoticed by God, I have learned. Dr. Nathanson's talk was instrumental in my willingness to finally forgive myself for the murder of my child. I had received absolution when I joined the church but the horror of many of my sins, particularly the abortion haunted me. At the suggestion of a Catholic friend, I had read Pope John Paul's *The Gospel of Life* with fascination. The man I had referred to as a troglodyte just five years ago wrote powerfully and persuasively as he argued against the evils of euthanasia, contraception, and abortion. But I was riveted when I read these words, they had been written to me:

I would now like to say a special word to women who have had an abortion. The Church is aware of the many factors which may have influenced your decision, and she does not doubt that in many cases it was a painful and even shattering decision. The wound in your heart may not yet have healed. Certainly what happened was and remains terribly wrong. But do not give in to discouragement and do not lose hope. Try rather to understand what happened and face it honestly. If you have not already done so, give yourselves over with humility and trust to repentance. The Father of mercies is ready to give you his forgiveness and his peace in the Sacrament of Reconciliation. To the same Father and his mercy you can with sure hope entrust your child. You will come to understand that nothing is definitively lost and you will also be able to ask forgiveness from your child, who is now living in the Lord. With the friendly and expert help and advice of other people, and as a result of your own painful experience, you can be among the most eloquent defenders of everyone's right to life. Through your commitment to life, whether by accepting the birth of other children or by welcoming and caring for those most in need of someone to be close to them, you will become promoters of a new way of looking at human life.

The phrase, "and you will also be able to ask forgiveness

from your child", had resonated in my head for weeks. But I had been unable to summon the guts to write the letter I knew I needed to write to her, asking for her forgiveness. Until that day, while listening to Bernard Nathanson explain that he had been the cause of over 75,000 murders. And that his decision to become a Roman Catholic occurred because there 'was no other place to go for forgiveness.'

That night, after sitting and staring at the blank screen of my computer for what seemed like hours as I tried to get up the guts to do this, I wrote my letter to Nicole, asking her to forgive her father and me for killing her. Within seconds of writing the salutation, "love, your mother," I saw a nine or ten-year-old blonde girl, smiling, playing with other children in a beautiful grassy field, filled with flowers. I knew exactly who she was.

Before we moved out west, I did a series of talks about abortion. About what I did and why. The most frequent question from the audience when I had concluded my talk was about therapy. How long had I needed psychological or psychiatric counseling to be able to stand there and talk about this? Not infrequently, the questioner was a priest.

Why am I a Catholic? That's easy. I became a Catholic because I was led here. There was no intellectual process or rational comparison of faiths, no list of pros and cons, nothing linear or logical. There was merely that recognition shouting out at me, THIS IS IT, stop here. No need to continue any further, knowledge that I had before seen only glimpses of in a poem, book or a place. A knowing I knew was out there. But like my Poteet Victory painting of Sunset at Red Gorge, this is awareness beyond words, too immense for words.

Could I have acquired this same sense of belonging and truth in other traditions?

Perhaps, if I were not the me who God had in mind when he

'knit me together in my mother's womb.' But Catholicism is the soil I need to grow, to learn, to be at peace with me and my world. Over the years, I have enjoyed learning about the great faiths and see truth in them all, but I am profoundly Christian. Wholeheartedly, I believe that Christ is the Truth, the Way, and the Life. The Catholic Church is the conveyance by which I get to Him.

CHAPTER FIFTEEN

Marriage in the Church

"MY HOPE FOR EACH of you is that by the end of this weekend, if he is not already, that Jesus Christ will be your best friend." The speaker was a Legion of Christ priest ending his welcome message to the thirty or so women who were attending the Ignatian silent retreat in upstate New York. St. Ignatius of Loyola is one of my favorite saints. The founder of the Jesuit order of priests was a soldier, and had been raised to be a courtier and diplomat for the crown of Spain. A lover of dance, elegant clothes, and women, the soldier had little room for religion or Christ until he was forced to.

When a French cannonball shattered his leg during his one-man defense of Pamplona, the French were so impressed by his bravery that they carried him on a litter back to his home castle of Loyola. So severely injured that he was bedridden and had read through his favorite stories, he picked up a book about the lives of the saints. Slowly, Ignatius began to reflect about his feelings after he read one of his books about chivalry and romance as compared with his feelings after reading spiritual material. Emptiness and dissatisfaction as compared to peace and contentment. I like to think of him as a man who fell in love with

Christ because he had nothing better to do.

Those words struck terror in my heart. Total unmitigated dread. *Best friend, Christ? You've got to be kidding.* I stared at the crucifix behind the priest as he blessed us and provided brief instructions for the remainder of the weekend. It was Friday night, we were at this silent retreat until Sunday afternoon. My mind reeled with alarm and panic. *What if he asks me to leave John, become a hermit or take on some kind of dreadful disease?*

Unable to think or sleep most of that night, I thought only about how afraid I was of this suffering Christ, how shamed by what I had done. In talking with John a few times about these recurrent thoughts, he had said once that despair was considered a sin. The opposite of the theological virtue hope, despair signified that your pride was so great that you believed yourself to be the worst sinner ever. John's comment certainly got my attention, but it was many years before I was able to consider Christ, my best friend.

One of my spiritual directors offered an explanation. Father Roland was Pastor at St. Mary's Church in Putnam Connecticut and during one of our weekly meetings, said, "Lin, we are redeemed, sinners. Bought and paid for by the blood of Christ." As a member of Regnum Christi, I had several duties, one of which was weekly spiritual direction and confession. Although many spiritual directors are not priests, I was drawn to certain pastors to ask them if they would agree. Father Roland and I had been meeting for six weeks or so, long enough for him to get a read on me. "I find there are two kinds of Catholics. The first type emphasizes the redeemed part of that equation by ignoring sin, the other, usually converts, like you, focus on the sinner side of that equation."

This Catholic Christian world felt like another planet in another universe. Because I felt like such a novice in this faith, when a casual acquaintance, a psychiatrist friend of John's invited me to attend a Regnum Christi meeting with her on a Saturday morning, I went. It was a meditation on the book of Hosea led by one of the consecrated women in Regnum Christi. The soft cadence of her Irish accent echoed through the quiet room as she read from what she called the love story between God and humanity: The Old Testament.

> Yes, it was I who taught Ephriam to walk,
> I took them up into my arms;
> But they did not know that I healed them.
> I led them with cords of compassion,
> With the bands of love,
> And I became to them as one
> Who eases the yoke on their jaws
> And I bent down to them and fed them.

She was reading chapter eleven from the Book of Hosea; I had read it last summer. At John's suggestion, I had read the entire Bible. But in those lilting words, there was a love I had never perceived as I raced through the Old and the New Testaments. I became a member that morning. I doubt that I was the only woman wiping away tears as we listened to this holy woman share her wisdom.

Some of the women I met there and at other Regnum Christi meetings who now are my best friends are people I'd have rebuffed in my other life. Many, perhaps most, had always known what they wanted in life: Husband, children, family. Very like my Mom and sisters.

For the five years we lived on the East Coast, I maintained an active membership in the organization.

The almost military structure provided by the group was essential to me in those early years. Although the Clinton, Massachusetts 'apostolate' group that I was assigned to was an hour drive away now that we were living in Connecticut, I tried never to miss those meetings. Held in the home of the Philbin sisters, Eleanor and Marguerite provided steadfast guidance, love and mentorship to each of us as we gathered to pray and meditate in their living room each week.

While doing a 'whole life confession' with a Legionary priest during a Regnum Christi weekend retreat, my sobs turned to laughter when the priest interrupted and said, "Read *Men Are From Mars, Women Are From Venus.*" My hilarity hit because one of my last conversations with Randy had been his strong suggestion that I read that book. One which I considered insulting, the book was psychobabble, had to be. And hearing this holy priest instruct me in his thick Spanish accent to read it for my penance struck me as hilarious.

But once I picked up author John Gray's book, I felt as if I were reading about my husband and me. *Why had it taken me so long to get it? The missed cue and, errors were legion!* All of those years, telling myself and others that the only differences between men and women were anatomic and physiological. What rubbish and yet so many of us believe it. Still.

The militant nature of the group was off-putting for some Regnum Christi members, I was occasionally told, but it fit me and my former life perfectly. The notion of life as combat was familiar, switching the metaphor to spiritual combat was a piece of cake. And the idea of a spiritual plan to fight our individual temptations suited my need for a structured approach to my spiritual life.

It was the Cathedral of St Patrick in Norwich Connecticut where I saw the light for the third time. Taking advantage of every opportunity, I had joined a group at our local parish which promised to enhance the gifts of the Holy Spirit. A several month course during which we shared prayer, meditation and talk, the class ended with a Sunday afternoon celebration at the Cathedral. Diane, a friend from UMass and I had taken the course together, enjoying the people we met along with the tangible effects in our prayer lives. This celebration consisted of a ceremony where we joined the Bishop on the altar of the beautiful Neo-Gothic church. I could not concentrate on anything that he said because of the intense light that emanated from the apex of the altar. I was squinting and sweating because of the heat radiating from it.

Diane and I had talked almost non-stop until we got to my house. As we started up into the house, I remembered and said, "I just wish they hadn't had that searchlight up there, I was so distracted I could not focus on anything that was happening."

"What light?"

"Don't tell me you did not notice that light, Diane."

Laughing now, she said, "There was no searchlight there, Lin, you saw the light of the Holy Spirit. No, I did not see it."

The parting from UMass was peaceable. They had asked, and I'd agreed to stay on through the early phase of the merger with Memorial to help with the major budgetary changes which would hit the system and the managers with massive changes. That 'departure phase' lasted over six months which worked well for them and me.

For several reasons, we decided to come out west in 2002. After purchasing a house in a remote valley in northern Nevada, we have been here ever since. John had taken early retirement from his job as a psychologist with the Veterans Center, and our small online marketing business was remarkably profitable. Both of us enjoyed the freedom of working from home and were captivated by the beauty of the high desert. Although I enjoyed the learning about sales, the internet, and details of the business that only a small business owner can appreciate, I missed writing. The self-help books I had written about marketing and sales helped that need, but I knew something was missing.

During a trip to Italy with John, I discovered just what that was. Since our early married years, John had told me how much he wanted me to see Italy, He and a friend had gone there years before, and he knew that I would love the country, Rome, Florence, the Uffizi, the Vatican, Assisi. All of it.

Of course, I did. Who could not fall in love with that beautiful country, its vibrant citizens, and magnificent cathedrals? But of all of them, including St. Peter's, it was the Chiesa del Jesu, the mother church of the Jesuit Order, that I was swept off my feet by.

Over and over during the five days, we were in Rome, I would ask that we go there. Only during the last time, I would see that church did I take notice of the black coffin which holds the remains of St. Ignatius of Loyola. Excited for no reason I could state, I went over to the pew which tracks the length of the coffin and begged. My prayers were answered in the middle of the next night in Zurich. The basic plot, title, and a few characters appeared in my head. Fiction, really?

CHAPTER SIXTEEN

The Desert

IT WAS ON A long hike in the mountains behind our house when the name and visual picture of a woman named Lindsey McCall appeared in my head. She was a cardiologist and cardiovascular researcher, and I could not get her out of my head. For months, the name and the woman kept popping into my mind, usually on those hikes. Only after that prayer in Rome, in the Chiesa, de Jesu did I get it. I was to write a novel about her. Once I completed it, John asked how I felt.

"I miss these people! Really miss them, for so long, they have a part of my psyche and even heart, does that sound insane?"

"Well, then why don't you write another book about them?" Now, why didn't I think of that?

For so many years, I had written non-fiction. And had completely forgotten my early dreams of writing novels. Until those hikes and those prayers. Writing that first novel required returning to Houston first for research, then for promotion once it was published. During the first trip for research, my friend Margaret was kind enough to come to Mass with me at St. Vincent de Paul Church on Buffalo Speedway, a church I had never noticed during the seventeen years I drove by it each day on the way to work in the medical center. Churches held no attraction to me back then. Margaret and I were also able to attend a daily Mass at the stunning Co-Cathedral of the Sacred Heart in downtown Houston. With a stained glass window of the Risen Christ which seems to flood the city with grace when viewed at night.

Perhaps two of the highlights of those trips were seeing Randy, the lawyer I had lived with for ten years and later Lynn, the woman who had asked that I leave Hermann. These were highlights because I understood the magnitude of the changes God has wrought in me. All of that emotion of that tumultuous summer was gone. I was able to be happy for each of them and know that that part of my past is dead. Forgiveness. One cannot overestimate the power of it.

The term 'Big Sky' fits the high Sierra landscape of northern Nevada. After living most of my life at sea level, in cities, the absolute stillness of our home at the base of the Pinion Mountains provides fertile territory for prayer, spiritual growth and yes, writing. The first few years we lived here, the precipitation was so scant that it the area felt almost incompatible with life. And yet, once I looked closely, I could see the horned lizards or horny toads which resemble the crushed granite so completely that over and over I would step in surprise when a clutch of gravel would gain legs and scamper away. The jack rabbits looking for all the world like someone's dour grandfather are as big as cats with enormous ears and the mountain lions living in the mountains are some of the most majestic creatures I have ever seen.

This is definitely the high desert. Only walking out to the end of the driveway, turning right, the dogs and I head up and up to thousands and thousands of acres of BLM land where we can hike this trail for hours and see no other people. One late July evening, either the first or the second year we lived here, realizing the dogs had had no exercise that day, I took them up the mountain path because it was finally cooling down.

On the way back down, I just happened to look to my right to see a huge golden head with piercing emerald colored eyes staring at us. The lion must have been standing on some kind of promontory, but I could see the details of the face, whiskers, and fearless eyes so clearly that I was stopped. And merely stood to stare paralyzed. Until one of the dogs followed my gaze and began to trot over to where the beautiful animal stood, watching. *That is a mountain lion, move and quickly!* Hissing out an order of come and praying that he would respond, I turned back to the trail and headed back home at a good clip. A valuable lesson: This is the territory of the mountain lions, coyotes, and bears. No longer do I hike in the evenings.

This land is not for everyone. Too dry, remote and stark. But for those of us willing to live in the almost surreal landscape of sagebrush, rabbit brush, black widows, and rattlesnakes, the mystical gifts are prodigious. I think Christ must love the desert because it is here where I have received direction, consolation, and inspiration. Having talked with plenty of devout Catholics and heard the opinions of some priests in the matter, I know that there are more than a few who would consider the voices or what St. Teresa of Avila called locutions, that I hear with some frequency, auditory delusion or fantasy. And perhaps they are correct about some of them. But not all. I think it's more a matter of expectation.

Let me explain.

When I read Teresa of Avila's three books: her autobiography, *Interior Castle* and *Way to Perfection*, I believed what she wrote when she said that divine union with 'His Majesty' or Christ can be achieved by each of us. Not because I am holier than others, not that at all but just because it makes no sense to me that the persons of the Trinity would not answer us when we seek wisdom, direction or solace. Or that only the prophets of the Old Testament were able to hear the voice of God. So I am no longer surprised when fully formed thoughts appear in my mind, thoughts which sound like a voice while at prayer or during a hike. St. John explains that we must 'test the spirits.' Early on I learned to do this. When I hear in response, "I AM who AM." I need nothing more to know who is speaking to me.

There have been a few times where I have been told to do something that I had not planned to do. And after doing so, being wholly clueless about why I was to do this. Like, fly alone to Medjugorje half-way across the world. Or travel to the impoverished Colonias about thirty miles southeast of Tijuana, Mexico.

After reading a book about the apparitions of Mary to three teenaged girls in the then Communist-controlled town of Medjugorje while we were still living on the east coast, the idea of traveling there to the site of the apparitions began to appear in my head. I successfully ignored them until we moved here and learned that a group from the church where we generally attended Mass were planning a trip that next fall. As it turned out, the group had to cancel their planned pilgrimage until the following year, but I knew if I put it off I would not do it.

Meeting and staying at the house of Mirjana Dragicevic-Soldo was pure privilege. She had been sixteen when on a summer vacation from her home in Sarajevo, she first saw and hear Our Lady on June twenty-fourth and has received monthly apparitions from her each month. Married with two daughters, she hosts pilgrims like me and the twenty or so others in the group I was with.

For ten days, our group slept in groups of four in her home that she had turned into a dormitory and ate dinner in her huge kitchen. I had no doubt about the truth of Mirjana's visions but had hoped to hear or see some of my own. It seemed that almost all of my fellow pilgrims saw extraordinary things, but I saw nor felt nothing. A woman who stayed across the hall from the room in which I slept had been there eleven times, each year, she brought new women with her. Because she explained to me, 'I need an annual Medjugorje fix."

But the journey felt like a complete waste of time and money to me because, by the fifth day there, I called John to tell him that I thought I had made a huge mistake. Surrounded by people 'falling in the spirit', seeing the sun spin and a number of extraordinary phenomena, I could not even pray. In fact, the emptiness I felt frightened me. I wondered if I was losing my faith. John's reply? "That's a good thing, you don't need supernatural signs to believe. Don't worry."

A few years later, following a ten day trip to the poorest of the poor in Mexico, I felt the same confusion about why I had made that trip and what it had accomplished. Maybe one day, I'll know.

Shortly after I returned from Mexico, I joined the Benedictine Oblate group at St. Gall's Church in Garnerville. Although the church is close to a one-hour- drive from home, I had missed the structure afforded by Regnum Christi to my prayer life. The Oblate group in Nevada seemed to provide enough but not too much structure. Made up of lay-people, we Oblates live as monastics in the world. Praying the Divine Office three times per day and reading through the Rule of St. Benedict three times each year.

When I joined the church at St. Benedict's Abbey, I had never heard of Benedictine Oblates. And when I read the Rule of St. Benedict each day I can vividly remember purchasing a copy of the Rule at the Abbey in Massachusetts. Only to find that I understood not one word of it. It felt like just another foreign language. So did the psalms that I read at John's suggestion early in our friendship. I did read the Bible in its entirety that first year, but much of it was opaque even incomprehensible to me. The vocabulary of faith, initially alien, over time, food. Many of those psalms and Gospel passages I have committed to memory, I love them so dearly. Here is one of my favorites:

> It is good to give thanks to the Lord,
> to make music to your name, O most High,
> to proclaim your love in the morning
> and your truth in the watches of the night,
> on the ten-stringed lyre and the lute,
> with the murmuring sound of the harp.
>
> Your deeds O Lord, have made me glad;
> For the work of your hands I shout with joy.
> O Lord, how great are your works!
> How deep your designs!
> The foolish man cannot know this
> and the fool cannot understand.
>
> The just will flourish like the palm tree
> And grow like a Lebanon cedar.
> Planted in the house of the Lord
> They will flourish in the courts of our God,
> still bearing fruit when they are old,
> still full of sap, still green,
> to proclaim that the Lord is just;
> to him, my rock, there is no wrong.

All human emotion is reflected in the one-hundred fifty psalms attributed to David and sung daily through the ages as laments or praise to God. In my daily Office, there are times when I feel the presence of all those voices who sang before me.

CHAPTER SEVENTEEN

The So-what of Faith

I STAND FIRMLY ON mystery, on what I do not understand. I am paraphrasing what Julian of Norwich wrote centuries ago when writing those words, but she describes the life of faith thoroughly with those few words. Over much time and prayer, the rules of Catholicism have receded into the background, and my idea of sin has changed radically. I know now that sin, all sin, is an offense against Love.

A few years ago, I talked with Father Paul, my spiritual director about my inability to eradicate the many flaws in my personality. I felt that I confessed the same sins of impatience, anger, willfulness over and over again. He suggested to take them to God. So I did that. I made a list of all the characteristics of my nature that I dislike, filled an eight by eleven page and brought the page to Adoration. Prayer in front of the exposed Christ. And completing my list of flaws I wanted Him to take away, I stopped and was still. And then I heard laughter.

C.S. Lewis explains: *I think all Christians would agree with me if I said that though Christianity seems at first to be all about morality, all about duties and rules and guilt and virtue, yet it leads you on, out of all that, into something beyond. One has a glimpse of a country where they do not talk of those things, except perhaps as a joke. Everyone there is filled full with what we should call goodness as a mirror is filled with light. But they do not call it goodness. They do not call it anything. They are not thinking of it. They are too busy looking at the source from which it comes. But this is near the stage where the road passes over the rim of our world. No one's eyes can see very far beyond that: lots of people's eyes can see further than mine.*

We are not alone. Quite the contrary, we swim amidst an entire cloud of witnesses waiting to be invited into our lives. The Cathedral of Our Lady of the Angels Los Angeles was built amidst extensive controversy under then-Cardinal Roger Mahoney. The conflict involved a whole series of issues, primary among them is its ultra-modern design and stark architectural differences from its nineteenth-century predecessor. Upon our first visit to the Cathedral several years ago, John and I were riveted by the church. The space is cavernous, filled with light and high upon the stark white walls, hanging large murals depict the community of saints wholly recognizable. Teresa of Avila, St. Francis of Assisi, St. Jerome, Augustine, Thomas of Aquinas, Ignatius of Loyola, all there. A cloud of witnesses.

I think not infrequently of what Steve Linder told me during that kind and generous conversation following receipt of my doctorate. He had said that all the years of study had created an intellectual community of friends. Friends I would meet and recognize as I came upon their works again and again. The community of saints is like that. Heavenly friends ready and willing to intercede for us if we would just ask. Friends of Jesus, who can take our hand and lead us to him.

Early in the morning several years ago, both the dog and I were startled by hammering on the front door in the late afternoon. John was traveling, and when I opened the door, I was surprised to see the distraught face of our next-door neighbor, Karen. With spittle leaking out of each side of her mouth, she exclaimed, "Tell me that you are not one of those Christians who believe every word in the Bible is true. Tell me that an educated woman like you knows that most of that book is fantasy and fairy-tale." Refusing any invitation to come on and sit down, she kept repeating the same things until I said, "Karen, I do believe the Bible is the inspired Word of God. Yes, I do."

Shaking her head in disgust, she turned and walked back across the street to her house.

Faith is a lightning rod. And in the end, cannot be explained but lived. In those early years following my conversion, a woman I worked closely with, a self-proclaimed Jewish atheist, smiled one day while we talked and said, "I am the anvil to your hammer." I realized that day that my passion, my zeal could not open up a heart that was closed. No longer do I use reason or logic to bring someone back to faith. I know there is only one who can do that.

"So how is your life different, now that you are a Catholic?"

I've been asked that question numerous times over the last couple of decades. Each time, I hear the question, I take a deep breath mentally if not physically before I answer. It's a straightforward, ordinary question. And it should be an easy one to answer.

Yes and no. The last time I the question was posed was during an interview for a Catholic women's radio program, I said, "Everything is different, and nothing is different." The interviewer laughed somewhat uneasily during the still air filling the silent phone line. It wasn't a live interview, so there was no concern about dead air.

Speaking into the silence, I continued, "Remember the Zen maxim, or is it called a koan? 'Before enlightenment, chopping wood and carrying water. After enlightenment, chopping wood and carrying water.'" The words are modest, unassuming, but they describe precisely how my life felt before God and after. But perhaps its meaning is opaque to the many for whom faith has not been such a struggle, such a determined and long-term search. As is the case for that interviewer, my husband and most of the Christians both Catholic and not that I have talked with during the years since my conversion.

During the years far away from the church, I studied Buddhism. Mostly because I knew I needed to learn how to meditate. Working full-time at an all-consuming job while in pursuit of a doctorate in Public Health was not a recipe for sanity, I knew. So I subscribed to Tricycle Magazine and rose at four in the morning to do at least fifteen minutes of meditation before I began the reading for the courses I was taking at school. In one of the first magazines I read, that saying appeared. And instantly I recognized the truth of it." Before enlightenment, chopping wood and carrying water, after enlightenment, chopping wood and carrying water." I memorized it over twenty years ago because I recognized its truth.

Truth. Finally, I know Truth. And Truth is a person, not a religion, his name is Jesus Christ. That fact changes everything. And yet, outwardly, I look no different from the way I did before the return to church. The daily routines of life remain unchanged. Being a convicted committed Catholic does not preclude illness or pain. My faith doesn't insulate me from fights with my husband or the hurt from a stinging review of one of my books. Severe wind storms lash severely enough to uproot the most magnificent tree in our garden and knock enough shingles off the roof to require a costly replacement of the entire roof. Friends from my life before my conversion can be more distant, in some cases, disappear. The perceived changes too great for them to absorb.

But finally all of these years later, I can say to that Legionary priest, Yes, Jesus is my best friend. It took much more than that weekend, it took close to twenty years for me to get past the fear, soften my heart enough to hear him, receive him, accept his love.

Wisdom is the effulgence of light
The spotless mirror of the power of God
The image of Goodness
She who is one can do everything whilst herself perduring
Through the ages, she passes into holy souls
Producing friends of God and prophets.

CHAPTER EIGHTEEN

Conclusion

WRITING THIS BOOK HAS felt like a balancing act. While needing to explain how and why I walked away from God, working very hard to avoid page after page of 'all about me.' One Sunday morning I ruefully commented to John that I thought initially this return to non-fiction would be more or less of a no-brainer. After all, it's logical and linear: write the outline and then follow it. My psychologist husband replied that he thought this no easy task. "You need to write about yourself but must be careful about coming across as narcissistic. And you're talking about how and why you returned to God, faith, and the Catholic Church but have to be wary of coming across as 'holier than thou.' " He thought for a few more minutes then said, " No, I wouldn't believe that this is a simple book for you. Actually, I believe that this is most likely harder than writing the novels." And then he walked away to resume his daily battle with the stock market.

There's only one reason to write a book like this. In hopes of easing another's decision to return or turn for the first time to God and to Church. To find comfort and consolation in faith, religion and church whether it be Roman Catholic, Anglican, Judaism or any of the other traditions that point us toward God the Father. One of the few things about which I am certain is the personhood of Jesus Christ and his salvific role for you and for me. Therefore, the many other traditions which address methods and techniques to address happiness, reduction of stress and meditation have many beneficial effects. Among them, however, is not the salvation of our souls.

I recall clearly my introduction to Postmodernism. The head of my dissertation committee, also my advisor, and I were discussing the qualitative argument for what turned out to be my dissertation from Hell. Part of what I had been contending, Steve claimed, went right in line with Postmodernist theory. Utterly baffled by his phrase, I voiced my confusion, and he handed me a book written by a new faculty member at the school of Public Health. Inwardly groaning, for I should have known any question would have led to another book to read, I smiled a thanks. And scanned the book over the next several weeks so that I could return it.

"What do you think of Postmodernism?" he asked as he returned the book to the overflowing bookcase in his office.

I shifted uncomfortably in my chair as I looked at him. He was watching me with a studiedly neutral expression. "The underlying assumption seems to be that we can be sure of nothing. There are no truths or absolutes: ideas and principles are fundamentally circuitous thinking." Steve smiled very slightly but said nothing, just waited.

I took a deep breath. "I think the denial of all truth is absurd…"

Even in this twenty-first century, we must each determine our answers to questions like 'Who am I?' 'Why am I here?' 'Does God really exist?' 'Can there be any meaning in all of this suffering?' 'Why does God permit such evil?' The wording of the questions may vary from person to person, but the overall meaning is the same. There is an emptiness in chasing after whatever suits our current fancy, the satisfaction is never more than momentary.

Karl Rahner wrote in his classic text, *Foundations of the Christian Faith*, that "the Christian of the twenty-first century will be a mystic or nothing it all." In one of our early meetings, my spiritual director, Father Paul McCollum handed over his copy of Rahner's book to me during a conversation where he declared that the theologians were always in tension with the institution of the Church. "The theologians are the new prophets, continually causing unrest within the mainstream church. Rahner was one of the most influential theologians preceding the changes instituted by Vatican ll." Smiling, but without a lot of humor, Fr. Paul explained, "But some of his writing was too far-reaching, so he fell from favor shortly after that. I think you will enjoy Rahner."

I did. And made a new friend. Although much of Rahner's philosophy was difficult, even opaque, I worked my way through the tome in much the same way that I had with the Aquinas text borrowed from Brother Andrew years before. And when asked if I am a mystic, I smile as I recall Rahner's statement. Because he used the word mystic in its most radical sense. Without a long and academic explanation. For Rahner, a mystic is a person with a *real* experience with the Person of Christ. In that sense then, yes, I am a mystic. I hear his voice and have seen his spirit.

With the prescience of the prophet, Rahner wrote these words during the last century, living and writing throughout the horrors of Hitler's Germany. Along with another prophet from another tradition, martyr and Lutheran pastor Diedrich Bonhoeffer, Karl Rahner saw clearly the evils of the state, run amuck. Untrammeled evil. Worth repeating here: "The Christian of the twenty-first century will be a mystic or [she] will be nothing."

In our twenty-first century, we speak a new language. In this new dialect where sin is denied and euphemisms replace truths in the name of justice, tolerance and equality, Rahner and Bonhoeffer call out to us. Particularly women. For us women, there is danger in behaving exactly like men, in accepting the 'equality' now legislated by the government. In pursuing the sexual liberation afforded us by the cornucopia of contraceptive agents, we think we can jump from bed to bed with impunity. We leave landscapes littered with broken families and aborted babies. Although the sexual liberation decades ended long ago, the gender wars drag on into this twenty-first century.

Men and women are not equal. Our physiologies are different enough for us to know, deep down, that one another is an alien species, sexually, emotionally and in most other ways. But we now fight against this as if this fact were primitive and coarse. And it makes some of us angry, we women who want to be women but also to barge with impunity into formerly male bastions...like combat, where some men act like men, not women.

Our actions and decisions have consequences. When we join 'male-only' clubs we need to understand that we've moved to a different planet with a different language that we will never speak, no matter how hard we try. Most especially we see these differences during times of combat or extreme challenges.

Our naïve and simplistic notions of passing laws in the belief that legislation changes the nature of things, the makeup of men and women, is foolhardy. Culturally, we have confused ourselves and our children with our frantic attempts to declare that men can be women, even mothers, women can be men, even fathers, marry and use technology to form a family and call it natural. Resting in the protection of the law. Ignoring the consequences, blinding ourselves. As if it's a matter of equality between men and women. As if female West Point Cadets should be surprised by the assault of other male cadets while alone in the wilderness.

Or the outrage of female soldiers who get raped by male soldiers when certain men get the opportunity. Or me years ago, when I let a guy I dated into my bedroom, and he did not listen when I said no. Later, friends told me I should sue him...for 'date rape.' Really? When I let him into my bedroom, eyes wide open?

We ignore these troublesome problems at our peril. And the hell of it is that we cannot look to others for the answers, when we do, we just waste time, precious time. Without the answers, our own, not another's, we can find no authentic joy, peace or solace.

There is nothing extraordinary about me or my life. I am an ordinary woman who has lived an ordinary life. Although I have worked hard, many people work harder, although I am educated, there are millions far better educated than I will ever be. I say these things not to trivialize my gifts, for which I am exceedingly grateful, nor to undermine the work I have done. But rather to forestall the thoughts of a reader who makes excuses for not acting on the yearning she has for a closer relationship with Christ. Excuses I have heard my whole life, like, 'Lin is a genius, she is smarter, holier, worthier' the nonsense we tell ourselves while we justifying our inaction. This is no game. We are playing for keeps.

What *is* extraordinary is my story. And the potential consequences for you as you read my words.

A story of a young woman who lost her faith. Totally, completely, and absolutely. Who began to search over the next years and decades for what had been lost. Who now can tell you unequivocally she knows who she is and that God does exist. Who much of the time is flattened, crushed and astonished at the privilege of being in His Presence, whether at Mass, Adoration or merely walking along one of our high desert roads. This is a love story, very definitely. But one that tells about His love for you and for me. The astounding lengths He goes to bring us to Him. Each one of us with our personal, intimate and sometimes tragic journey. I will conclude with just such a story.

When I received my niece Terri's call that my older sister had been found dead, I was unsurprised. I had been expecting that call for many years. My sister Patty was incapable of happiness. She endured much of life by anesthetizing herself with drugs and alcohol. Patty's three children received the fallout from a mother who could not love herself.

"She's dead! Where is she?" Barely five in the morning, I had sleepily groped my way into my home office and picked up my private line. The one reserved for customers. Like a child, my forty-something niece was sobbing and repeating the same thing, over and over. I had no answer and could merely promise that I would be there as soon as I could get a flight out from Reno to Boston.

I had time to attend Mass on the way to the airport two days later. And knelt in the back of the church overcome by my self-disgust that my intense grief was for the sudden death of my Doberman just two weeks before. That my eyes were dry and my heart hollow at the thought of Patty's life and her death, alone with an empty gallon bottle of vodka and a couple of empty prescription bottles. My niece's question echoed in my mind as I knelt there, overcome by the assault of emotion I felt, not sorrow but a helpless kind of anger at the waste, at Patty's relentless self-destruction and its awful toll on her three children.

Quite clearly, as if the speaker were kneeling right beside me, Terri's question was answered.

"Patty is with me. Go and tell them how much I love them."

My sister, as far as I knew, did not attend church, did not believe in any of the religious trappings or doctrines of any religion. She had been particularly antagonistic toward the Catholic

Church for years. Resentful of the promise she had made when she married her Catholic ex-husband, to bring up their children as Catholics. And, my oldest sister Lee had once revealed, that Patty had been angry at me for becoming a Catholic, the religion she loved to hate. But I had no doubt about what I heard. Or what it meant.

My sister's son and daughter's had asked a minister from a nearby church to conduct their mother's Memorial Service. There were many of her friends at the service, about fifty or sixty people. When the minister asked if there were anything any of us wanted to say, I walked to the front of the room, looked at Terri and said, "I know where your mother is, Terri." And then proceeded to explain.

"Go and tell them how much I love them."

Now that *is* extraordinary.